The HERB TEA BOOK

Blending, Brewing for Every Moo...

SUSAN CLOTFELTER

Happy Sipping!

Susan Clotfelter

INTERWEAVE PRESS

Acknowledgments

This book would have been impossible without the patient and generous help of Doree Pitkin, Nancy Disney, Stephen Beal, Betsy Strauch, and especially Kathleen Halloran at Interweave Press.

Disclaimer

The contents of this book are not intended as a substitute for medical treatment, nor should they be used as such. Consult youir physician or other health-care practitioner in all matters affecting your health, and carefully follow the advice you receive.

Photo props courtesy of The Cupboard and Happenstance, both of Fort Collins, CO, and Fox Ryde Gardens, Loveland, CO.

Cover design: Elizabeth R. Mrofka
Book design: Dean Howes
Photography: Joe Coca Photography
Photo styling: Susan Strawn Bailey

Interweave Press, Inc.
201 East Fourth Street
Loveland, Colorado 80537-5655
USA

Printed in the United States of America

Library of Congress Cataloging-in-Publication Data

Clotfelter, Susan.
    The herb tea book : blending, brewing, and savoring teas for every
mood and occasion / Susan Clotfelter.
       p. cm.
    Includes index.
    ISBN 1-883010-60-8 (pbk.)
    1. Tea. 2. Herbal teas. I. Title.
TX817.T3C47 1998
641.3′ 372—dc21   98-34442
                                   CIP

First printing: IWP—10M:798:KP

To the tea formulators who contributed their recipes and enthusiasm;
to Mort and Jean Clotfelter, who chopped wood and carried water;
and to Martha, Jim, Sheron, and Curtis, who kept the fire from going out.

Contents

About Herbs

*n*early five thousand years ago, Chinese legend recounts, the first tea leaf drifted into a cup of boiling water. Since then, humans have sipped the infused virtues of tea. For all those centuries, courtesans with secret smiles, revolutionaries hatching plots, mothers tending sick children, sailors weathering a storm, and long-separated friends have gathered, cupping warmth in their hands, over tea.

It is likely that herb tea is at least as old. While tea, strictly defined, refers only to the processed leaves of *Camellia sinensis,* an evergreen shrub, herb tea can consist of various parts of other plants, occasionally in combination with tea leaves. This distinction aside, the friendship between herbs and tea is a venerable one. In fact, Shen Nong, the Chinese emperor believed to have drunk that first accidental cup of tea, is also credited with penning the world's earliest surviving herbal, *Pen Tsao Ching,* or *The Classic of Herbs.* (Shen Nong was also supposed to have lived for a thousand years and had a transparent abdomen, but never mind that.) As early as the Tang Dynasty (A.D. 618-906), the Chinese were adding flavorings to their favorite brew, among them salt, ginger, cloves, peppermint, orange peel and even onions.

In this book we ask you to celebrate this crossing of categories, to reunite herbs and tea. Already, in some of the most cherished and expensive teas available, *C. sinensis* flirts with the scents and flavors of flowering trees such as jasmine, peach, and plum. Why stop at flirtation? Why not just fire up the miniature jacuzzi and throw them in together?

While a reverence for fine tea is a good and noble thing, we want to encourage a spirit of playfulness and creativity in using it. No law forbids mixing a high-quality Dragonwell with rosemary or fresh lemon or tangerine zest; the tea police will not arrive to cite you. A holiday gift of rare Assam can be spiced with cardamom and ginger and mellowed with a dollop of half-and-half. Try fending off an oncoming cold by throwing some echinacea in your orange pekoe. Combining rare leaves from the fertile foothills of a land you may never see with flowers from the familiar garden of a friend is a fine way to savor the world.

Starting Out with Herb Tea

To experiment with blending tea herbs, you may first want to try brewing one herb at a time, to get a feel for the individual scents and flavors of herbs. Some tea herbs are tasty enough to go solo—chamomile, peppermint, and sage, for example. Others, like basil and thyme, may not be unpleasant, but are best when blended with other flavors. Some herbs, such as licorice, are strong and sweet enough to mask the taste of ingredients that are less palatable. When you begin mixing tea herbs, it helps to know as much as possible about the herbs and their histories, uses and tastes, and to also be aware of any side effects they may have, especially if you are under a doctor's care or taking any medication. This chapter includes very brief profiles of the herbs, spices, and other ingredients used frequently in this book. For more information about herbs, check the list of additional reading on page 126.

Drying, Buying, Blending, and Storing

Drying. If you have an herb garden, it is the freshest possible source of herbs for tea. If you garden, but don't plant herbs yet, we hope the teas in this book will inspire you to give herbs a try; many are among the easiest, most resilient plants to grow.

To dry herbs for tea, first be sure to harvest the required parts at their peak, before they are spent or have gone to seed. Wash or brush herbs to remove dirt and bugs, then tie into small bundles and hang them from the ceiling in a dark, but well-aired room. If the drying area is dusty or high-traffic, tie paper bags around the herb bundles, cutting small slits in the bags to prevent the contents from mildewing. Or spread out herb stalks on old, clean window screens to dry.

If your climate is *really* humid, you may have more success with faster drying methods. A gas stove with a pilot light will dry small herb bundles in two to three days. For the best, freshest-looking dried herbs, borrow or buy a food dehydrator.

Buying. When buying herbs for tea, remember that you're not limited to the bulk section of your local natural food store, although the selection and quality there may be excellent. Choose herbs that are still fragrant and colorful. Herbs that are in high demand may have a faster turnover and be fresher, while less common herbs may be stale and impart little flavor to your tea. The volatile oils in herbs evaporate quickly, especially when an herb is cut and sifted, exposing more surface area. However, dried roots, such as astragalus, are more convenient to buy already cut.

Mail-order suppliers may be able to bring fresher herbs to your doorstep than you can buy locally. They are often cheaper in larger quantities; share orders with a friend or make a batch of tea for gifts. If you're not satisfied with the quality of an herb that you receive by mail order, consult the vendor for a return.

Blending. Some of the teas in this book can be blended in quantity in advance, and the recipes are written to make this easier to do. If you want to blend more or less of a particular tea, simply scale the ingredients up or down proportionately. For teas that use fresh herbs, this isn't possible, although they can be brewed and then frozen for a few months, or refrigerated for up to three days.

The recipes in this book use dried herbs unless otherwise specified. Substituting fresh herbs for dried can be done in most teas and is usually worth a try. When substituting, use approximately three times as much fresh herb unless the recipe directs otherwise. Some herbs will simply taste more green and grassy; others, used fresh, will have a delicacy that is missing in the dried version.

Crumble, chop, or coarsely grind your ingredients to allow them to stay blended better, but don't powder them. Then store dried tea blends in a glass container away from light. Give the jar a good shake before removing a few teaspoons to make tea; this helps redistribute different-sized ingredients more evenly.

———

The volatile oils in herbs evaporate quickly, especially when an herb is cut and sifted, exposing more surface area.

———

Storing. Once dried, herbs and blended teas should be stored away from the light and the heat, just as tea itself should be. Glass containers are preferable, because plastic resealable bags still have some permeability. Ingredients for teas, or crushed spices on their way to becoming teas, especially seeds, roots and other woody parts, can be stored in the refrigerator or freezer. This is especially useful if your summers are hot and humid. Herbs, spices, and many teas will lose some to most of their flavor after storage for a year. Make a cup of tea to bid them farewell, and then compost or trash them.

Herbs and Safety

While many herbs work gently, it's important to remember they can also have dramatic and powerful effects, If you have allergies or a specific health challenge, or if you are on medication or pregnant, consult with your health care practitioner before using herbs in any form, even in tea. Most herbs that have common culinary uses are safe in the quantity contained in one cup of tea, but some individuals are sensitive to even these amounts.

Some of the teas in this book use essential oils for added flavor and fragrance. These oils are the concentrated active chemicals contained in the plants, so they must be used carefully and sparingly. Do not exceed the recipe amounts, and store *all* essential oils out of the reach of children.

Herbs for Tea

Aniseed. The seed of the anise plant is the source of flavoring for most licorice candy today, as well as many baked goods. Aniseed was known to the Egyptians and used to treat digestive disorders and toothache; in the Middle Ages the seeds were coated with sugar and taken after meals. Today they sweeten both tea and breath.

Basil. The herb so well-known after the pesto craze of the 1980s can be used in much more than Italian food. In tea, basil contributes savory notes that blend well with other herbs. This annual member of the mint family is easy to grow in a sunny spot in moist, rich soil. Try cinnamon or lemon basils if you are growing basil to use in tea.

Cardamom, a member of the ginger family, contributes pungent notes to many of the teas in this book, especially the chais. Each yellow-green pod contains about 20 brown seeds; some recipes call for the whole pod, others for the seeds. Used to make perfumes in ancient Europe, cardamom has yielded digestive medicines for centuries. It figures significantly in both Scandinavian and Indian cooking; Indians call it the "queen of spices."

Catnip is the same herb that sends felines into comedic spasms of joy. Humans, meanwhile, have found that it assists digestion and is gently calming. Catnip can even be used in teas for children. It's easy to grow at home—so easy that, like other mint family members, it may need to be contained..

Chamomile, one of the most common tea herbs, comes in two separate species: German (*Chamomilla recutita*) and Roman (*Chameaemelum nobile*). Flowers of the annual German chamomile are most often used for tea, since the Roman one gives a somewhat bitter taste. Chamomile's bright, daisylike flowers are as cheery as their infusion's golden color, the flavor of which is like drinking sunshine, some herbalists enthuse. Its antispasmodic and mildly sedative qualities make it a sovereign remedy for stomach upsets due to nervousness. However, some people who are allergic to ragweed pollen are allergic to the related chamomile.

Cinnamon is native to Sri Lanka, India, and Southeast Asia, but is cultivated throughout the tropics. The inner bark of an evergreen tree, it comes in dried sticks, chips or in ground form. For teas, buy cinnamon sticks and crush them yourself for a fresher flavor. Using the ground herb can yield muddy, overspiced tea.

Clove is an aromatic evergreen tree native to Indonesia. Its unopened flower buds are dried to make the familiar, brown, peg-shaped spice that flavors pumpkin pies and other holiday baking. Like cinnamon, cloves should be purchased whole and then coarsely crushed before using them in tea. Cloves are strong; if you're blending your own tea, go easy on them. Also, some people are allergic to cloves or find the flavor and smell irritating.

Dandelion root. The same long taproot that weeders curse for its tenaciousness, herbalists esteem as a diuretic and general cleansing herb. Roasted, it has an earthy flavor that makes it a good coffee substitute. To roast your own dandelion roots, scrub them well and roast in a 200-degree oven for about four hours, or until they are dark brown throughout. Grind and brew as for coffee.

Echinacea is one of the most popular herbal remedies today, often taken in capsules to stimulate the immune system's defenses against colds and infections. Two echinacea species (*E. angustifolia* and *E. purpurea*) provide a root with a multitude of beneficial chemical components. Both of these bright purple wildflowers can be grown at home, but as the root takes up to four years to develop, many gardeners choose to simply enjoy the flower's looks, and purchase their echinacea root for teas.

Fennel, a relative of the same bulb used as a vegetable in Mediterranean cooking, produces small, light green, ridged seeds that are a good digestive remedy. The flavor is akin to basil and anise, yet warmer, and is commonly found in sausage, curries and pickles. Indian cooks sometimes candy the seeds to chew after a meal.

Ginger root, native to tropical Asia, is now cultivated in the West Indies. This lumpy brown root gives a tangy bite to foods from stir-fries to gingersnaps and ginger ale. Fresh or dried, it is effective against stomach upsets from indigestion to morning and travel sickness. Use the dried, chopped root in tea blends; if you're making up just enough to drink right away, substitute the fresh root in roughly the same quantity for a more intense ginger flavor.

Hawthorn is a small tree or shrub whose berries and flowering tops have gained wide use both in the West and in Chinese herbalism as cardiac medicines. They are also high in bioflavonoids and antioxidants. In the United States, hawthorns are extensively grown as ornamentals.

Hibiscus flowers give many commercial teas a tart flavor and bright reddish color; the leaves and seeds are also edible. Rich in vitamin C and mildly antibacterial, hibiscus flowers are often combined with rosehips, another highly antioxidant herb.

Lemon balm leaves have a cheery, lemon scent most welcome on a gray day. Unfortunately, the fresh leaves available in summer are far tastier than the dried ones available during the rest of the year. The plant is easy to grow in moist soil and full sun. Lemon balm is the focus of research for its antiviral properties; it has long been used as a mood lifter, wound healer, and toothache soother.

Lemon verbena, a shrub that southern gardeners boast of but northern gardeners usually must pamper, is native to South America. Lemon verbena leaves give off a stronger and sweeter lemon scent than lemon balm, and they make marvelous tea. Although the plant can be challenging to grow in a cold climate, the scent of one crushed leaf is often reward enough for your trouble.

Lemon and **orange zest** and **peel** can be prepared at home for use in teas; simply scrape off the colored part of a citrus peel with a grater, potato peeler, or zester. Add to fresh teas, or dry and chop coarsely to add to dried tea blends. You can also experiment with other citrus peels—lime, tangerine, grapefruit, for example. These last three are astringent and tart; use a light hand or your tea will have too much pucker power.

Licorice root contains a substance that is fifty times sweeter than sugar, so its ability to sweeten teas is not surprising. Its anti-inflammatory qualities have been used to relieve many kinds of stomach upset, even ulcers. Pregnant women and those with high blood pressure or heart or liver disorders should not use it, however.

Peppermint and spearmint are so familiar, so well-loved and widely cultivated that a description is almost unnecessary. Cooling and sweet, these mints form the basis for many digestive teas, and can be added in smaller quantities to any tea for flavor or garnish. Because mint's many varieties are so easy to grow that containing them is advisable, they're the lazy gardener's favorite. One tea in this book uses orange mint, but it's fun to experiment with any strong-flavored mint in tea.

Rose petals and rosehips. Both the luxurious petals and hard, bright fruits of several rose species are used in teas. Rose petals imbue them with a soft, flowery scent and faintly sweet taste. Be sure to use only unsprayed petals or purchase certified organics. Rose hips are packed with vitamin C, and are often combined with hibiscus flowers for a rosy-colored tea.

Rosemary, famed for its many culinary uses, gives a clean, refreshing, piney scent and flavor to teas. It has long been believed to improve concentration and memory; the medieval herbalist Gerard wrote that it "comforteth the hart and maketh it merie." Aromatherapists today use it for the same purpose—to ease stress and lift mild depression. In areas with a Mediterranean climate, rosemary plants can become huge shrubs. In colder areas, they often need to be overwintered indoors.

Sage and pineapple sage are two different species in the mint family. Garden sage is the herb that's ubiquitous in turkey stuffing; pineapple sage is a red-flowered, fruity-flavored herb that makes a wonderful iced tea. Garden sage is valued as a remedy for sore throats and poor digestion, but it also makes a mineral-packed tea.

Scented geraniums (pelargoniums), though related to the familiar, big-flowered bedding plants, have modest, delicate blooms. Their foliage, however, is bounteously scented with a wild variety of fragrances. The fresh leaves of the various rose, mint, or citrus-scented cultivars are a tasty and fragrant addition to tea.

Siberian ginseng, sometimes labeled eleuthero, is not a true ginseng, but *Eleutherococcus senticosus*, a ginseng-like plant native to eastern Russia, China, Korea, and Japan. Herbalists use it to improve both physical and mental stamina; it's also thought to stimulate the immune system.

Skullcap in herbal recipes may be either American skullcap, *Scutellaria lateriflora*, or a species used in Chinese medicine, *Scutellaria baicalensis*, also called baical skullcap or huang qin. In teas, the leaves, stems and flowers of

American skullcap help calm nervous tension. Use American skullcap for the tea recipes in this book, but be careful to purchase only the cultivated herb from a reliable source; several years ago, adulteration with other herbs was a problem with skullcap. The herbalists who have used skullcap in this book say that the purity of American skullcap is now much more reliable, largely because of self-monitoring efforts by the herb industry.

Star anise is the eight-pointed woody fruit of an evergreen tree native to China, India, and Vietnam; the Chinese know it as "eight-horned fennel" and use it in five-spice powder. Its pungent flavor mixes well with other spices for aromatic teas such as chai and holiday concoctions.

Stevia has long been used by the Guarani people of Paraguay to sweeten their bitter drink, maté. This tender member of the verbena family can be grown as a houseplant. In some of the teas in this book, stevia provides its characteristic sweet qualities, making the addition of sugar unnecessary. If you like your tea sweeter than that produced by these recipes, increase the amount of stevia cautiously; stevia powder is roughly eight times sweeter than sugar, and powdered stevia extract much more so.

Common thyme and **lemon-scented thyme** lend a pungent aromatic flavor to teas, common thyme being a bit more medicinal tasting. The essential oil contained in thyme is also strongly antibacterial, so herbalists recommend teas containing thyme for the symptoms of coughs and colds. Herb gardeners wax poetic about thyme; it's easy to grow if it gets lots of sun and excellent drainage.

Vanilla is Spanish for little pod, and these long, narrow bean pods were appropriated by the Spanish when they found Montezuma's subjects using them in sixteenth-century Mexico. Vanilla extract is simply vanilla beans, bruised or chopped and soaked in alcohol, so it's easy to make your own. Soak the beans in a small amount of inexpensive vodka until the vodka has absorbed the vanilla's rich, sweet flavor.

Wintergreen is a familiar flavor in candies and gums, and comes from a native North American creeping evergreen shrub. It was a popular herbal remedy with Native Americans and a common substitute for tea during the American Revolution. Here it is used in teas mainly for its flavor and its digestive benefits. It should not be consumed, however, by those who are sensitive to aspirin.

About Tea

ost of the herbs in this book are either used fresh, or simply harvested and dried. But the leaves of *Camellia sinensis*—the only plant that yields what is strictly defined as tea—go through a variety of more complex processes before taking a swim in your teapot. These processes are inextricably entwined with the history of tea.

The Chinese began deliberate planting of *C. sinensis* around A.D. 300. Tea filtered into trade with the Turks in the next century; soon fancy tea wares were being exported for sale to the upper classes and laws were introduced to control the growing and harvesting of the leaves. Tea destined for export was steamed, crushed, and mixed with plum juice to form a paste, which was then compressed into cakes and baked. To brew tea, the cakes were roasted until they softened, then crushed to a powder that would yield a green beverage. The Japanese were buying tea in this form from the Chinese as early as A.D. 729.

All of this tea was still what would be called green tea today. After the fourteenth century, however, as tea began to be exported to more distant countries, its vendors needed a way to preserve its qualities for a longer period of time. It was found that allowing the newly plucked leaves to oxidize in humid air until they turned red, then halting the process by applying heat, would give the leaves a longer shelf life and a stronger liquor—the brew now known as black tea. The process of allowing the leaves to oxidize was called fermentation, although the leaf is actually decomposing, not fermenting. The misnomer for the process is still used in the tea industry.

Today, tea is cultivated in India, Pakistan, Nepal, Sri Lanka, Japan, parts of Africa and parts of South America. Hand pickers or mechanical harvesting machines trim two leaves and a bud from the plant's new growth. As with wine grapes, annual weather variation and regional soil conditions affect the quality and taste of the tea harvested. Also as with wine, there are many different ways of categorizing tea. Varieties of tea may be named for their particular tea-growing region, then for the specific plantation or tea-growing company within that region. Finally, a specific type of tea from an individual plantation may have a name of its own.

Green and black are not the only colors tea comes in. White tea, produced in China and Sri Lanka, is the least-processed type of tea. It is steamed and then gently dried; once brewed it is pale and very delicate in taste.

Oolong teas are made from leaves that have been withered, then gently rolled to bruise only the edges, which turn reddish in the same oxidation process used in black teas. Formosa oolongs are allowed to oxidize for a longer period than China oolongs.

Some teas are packaged as whole-leaf teas; others are chopped or broken into smaller pieces that can be processed into tea bags. Still other teas are blended with flower petals or flavoring oils to make floral-scented or flavored teas. Pu-Erh tea is black tea inoculated with a specific bacterium and compressed into shapes, often small, hollow balls. It is hard to find outside of China, where it is famed as a digestive aid.

Tea Blends

What do these kinds of teas have in common with the little white bags available in the supermarket? Tea in tea bags is most often a blend of several harvests from several areas. Tea bags were invented about the turn of the century and were originally cloth bags. Today's single-cup, filter-paper tea bags usually require tiny bits of leaves, called "fannings," and even smaller pieces known as tea dust, both for ease in manufacturing and quick infusion.

Most of the caffeinated teas sold at grocery stores are blends of various types. Blended teas offer the advantage of consistent quality and taste across inconsistent harvests. Specific types of blends have specific purposes and tastes. English and Irish breakfast blends, for example, are strong black teas, designed to stand up to milk and sugar, the way most Britons take their tea. Earl Grey is a black tea blend flavored with oil of bergamot. The famous Lipton tea is named for Thomas Lipton, a grocery millionaire who, after a visit to Ceylon (now Sri Lanka) in the late 1800s, realized that growing his own tea there and selling it at home in England could widen his profit margins. Russian Caravan, another common blend, usually contains Lapsang Souchong, a type of oolong tea that gives the blend a characteristic smokiness supposed to evoke campfires and camel caravans—the way tea originally was transported to Russia.

Several tea-growing regions produce types of teas that bear their names. Here are a few.

Assam. When the first Opium War broke out between Britain and China in 1839, the British Empire was already looking for alternative sources for the tea its citizens couldn't live without. It was found that Upper Assam in northern India already had some

C. sinensis growing wild. Assam is a strong, full-bodied, copper-red tea that takes well to milk and sugar.

Ceylon tea pays homage to the former name of its home, Sri Lanka. The strength of its flavor lies somewhere between Darjeeling and Assam.

Darjeeling tea takes its name from another tea-growing region in India, a very mountainous one centered around the town of Darjeeling at 6,500 feet. Since the climate, including rainfall and sunshine amounts, varies widely, Darjeelings also vary in taste and quality. They are medium-strong teas, often with an aftertaste compared to fruit, almonds, or muscatel.

Nilgiri, a lesser-known Indian tea, is grown in the mountains near the Indian Ocean. It's a softer tea, similar to Ceylon, and can be steeped for a long time. It's also the tea most often used for chai, a sweet, spicy, milky Indian tea drink.

Gunpowder tea, also known as pearl tea, is green tea that is rolled into small pellets or balls. The compact pellets keep well, better than most teas. This is the tea most often used in the Muslim world for mint tea.

Dragonwell is China's most renowned type of green tea, of which the finest grades are still made by hand. If you're going to become a tea connoisseur, fine Dragonwells are a good place to begin.

When you enter the world of specialty teas, you'll find that it's difficult to divine tea quality from browsing a mail-order catalog and even more difficult to judge taste from a rack of closed tins at a specialty store. The only way to find tea that you enjoy, and that does justice to the herb teas you blend at home, is to experiment by buying small amounts, brewing and sharing. In fact, the drinking of tea can be a marvelous vehicle for armchair travel. It can take you to Cameroon, Malawi, the mountains of Nuwara Eliya in Sri Lanka or the Nilgiri hills in the south of India. Cup in hand, you can explore China's seventeen tea-growing provinces and their individual plantations, and decide for yourself whether the trip was worth the ticket. While tea from famed plantations can be costly, as with wine, lesser-known, high-quality bargains are plentiful, and the adventure of discovery can be an irresistible lure.

Tools, Toys, and Techniques

Chop wood. Carry water. This is almost all you need to do to make tea.

Of course, like anything else, tea making invites complication, and it has had thousands of years in which to do it. As tea once again climbs in popularity, more and more tea gadgets are being marketed. Most of them are unnecessary. To make tea, your tools at their most basic will include a source of hot water, a receptacle in which to combine hot water and tea, and a way of filtering the leaves and other herbal material.

Sources of heat are beyond the scope of this book; use whatever you fancy—gas, electric range, propane, a fire. One decades-old tea gadget that is useful is the electric kettle. These appliances bring water just to the boiling point, then turn off automatically. Russell Hobbs and Cuisinart are two manufacturers of such kettles. If you drink a lot of tea, they can be a good addition to your paraphernalia, a bit costly (around $70) but worth the investment.

Pots and cups. When it comes to a teapot, there are only two cardinal rules: It must please you, and it must not drip. You can get a teapot shaped like anything you admire—your dog, the head of your favorite politician, kitchen appliances, designer vegetables, motorcycles.

You can spend thousands or a few thin dimes, and gloat over your extravagance or your thrift. Your pot can come from Portmeieron or Poughkeepsie. But if it leaks, you will curse it. You will be forever mopping counters and trays and friends' tea-stained laps. Your tea will become an aggravation instead of an oasis. If you're shopping at a flea market, bring a bottle of water and ask to test the teapot for leaks and drips.

The looks of your tea wares should delight you; whether that delight is aesthetic or perverse, educated or ignorant makes no difference to the tea. Some tea connoisseurs swear by glass teapots, others by English porcelain. Mug or pot should hold heat well; there's nothing more annoying than having to constantly microwave tea. If you brew single cups of tea often, a large cup with its own cover will come in handy; so will a saucer for holding a spent tea bag or wet spoon.

The Chinese have created several useful types of tea-brewing tools: the *guywan* or covered cup; Yixing earthenware teapots; and the thimble cups and other special teaware used in the Chinese ceremony of brewing black tea. The Japanese tea ceremony, *Chanoyu*, has even more specialized equipment and rituals. These traditional items can be hard to find in the

United States, but can be mail ordered. For more information about their history and how to use them, James Norwood Pratt's *The Tea Lover's Companion* (Birch Lane Press, 1996) is an invaluable resource.

Some tea aficionados are purists about the shape of a cup—to them, only the shallow, wide-bowled, tapering cups with delicate handles are teacups; everything else is a coffee cup. On the other hand, in the Middle East mint tea is usually served in small glasses, with or without handles. A complete British tea service, with matching teapot, sugar bowl, creamer, and tray to present it all on, can be a joy to own. Once again, the choices are yours; you can try the tea accessories and ceremonies of many countries, or develop your own ritual for tea.

Filters. Straining tea is not essential; whole tea leaves often sink to the bottom of a cup, allowing tea drinkers to sip their tea right off the top. The remaining leaves can be read to divine your future if you're so inclined. With a mixture of herb material, however, some plant parts are likely to float; this is especially true of some fresh herbs. So various methods of straining tea have been developed. If you brew a whole pot, you can simply strain each cup as you pour; most of the plant material will remain in the pot. If cleaning loose tea dregs from your teapot seems arduous or the chance of sipping stray plant parts is unattractive, many types of tea infusers are available. These tea cages should be as large as can fit in your mug or teapot, because good tea needs room to swim. Avoid tiny infusers in novelty shapes; they'll crowd your tea. An infuser for use in one cup should have at least twice as much room as is taken up by a heaping teaspoon of dry tea. If you're fastidious about drinking plant bits, choose the finest stainless steel mesh you can find.

Other tools. One gadget, stolen from coffee lovers, that tea drinkers may want to try is the French coffee press. A glass carafe with a plunger and mesh screen, the French press is good at removing floating herb and tea bits and also gives the steeped herbs a little squeeze.

Another tool that anyone making herb teas should own is a mortar and pestle for crushing hard

French coffee press

spices. Many seeds and barks, such as cumin, cardamom and cinnamon, fade quickly once ground. Buy these spices in their whole form, store in a cool dry place, and grind your own as needed. Mortar and pestle sets are sold in marble, glass, porcelain, and sometimes wood versions; the wood ones usually are too soft to be much use in crushing hard spices and seeds. You can also grind spices in an electric coffee grinder.

Techniques. First, consider the water. If you don't like the flavor of your tap water, or know it to have impurities, consider using bottled spring or mineral water or investing in a water purifier for the kitchen sink. Water pitchers with charcoal filters in the top are available and fairly inexpensive.

Warm your teapot, cup, or other brewing receptacle by filling it with very hot to boiling water. Allow this water to sit in the receptacle a few minutes while you make other tea preparations. Empty the receptacle just before you add boiling water and tea.

Be sure to use the appropriate water temperature. Most of the teas in this book specify just-boiled water. This means bring the water meant for tea to a rolling boil, then immediately remove it from the heat and pour it over your tea right away. For green teas, back off on the temperature; 170 to 185 degrees Fahrenheit is about ideal. And start out with cold fresh water; re-boiled water can give a flat-tasting brew.

Steeping times vary depending on the plant material being steeped. Black teas infuse more quickly than green; aerial parts of herbs, or the softer leaves, flowers and stems, infuse more quickly than roots, barks and berries. In some recipes, woody plant parts require long simmering to extract the necessary flavors; herbalists call the result a decoction (as opposed to an infusion, in which the materials are merely steeped). For chais and some other teas, a decoction is first produced, then more tea or herbs are steeped in the hot decoction.

Finally, enjoy your tea. Take time to sniff it, roll it around on your tongue, savor it. It is your creation, but also one that partakes of a rich tradition of contemplation and relaxed refreshment. Tea, especially herb tea, remains yin to coffee's yang, a brief respite in a rushed world. Honor that tradition. Have another cup.

Real Men Drink Tea

By Robert K. Henderson

For a nation whose birth cry was a costumed act of vandalism protesting the price of tea, American men are strangely ambivalent on the beverage today. While working-class guys in China, India, Japan, and the U.K. quaff tea of various colors by the thermosful, American men write it off as wimp juice. It's an historical riddle, really. The mere suggestion that tea might be unmanly would have prompted those paint-smeared, buckskin-clad Bostonians of yesteryear to heave the skeptic into the harbor along with the chests of top-grade pekoe. But their suit-and-tie-wearing male descendants fear the stuff. How did men fall so far?

It's tempting to pin tea's unpopularity in America on coffee. As a he-man beverage, coffee brings a lot to the party. It looks bad. It tastes bad. It smells . . . okay, it smells pretty good. But coffee boasts up to four times the caffeine of black tea, as well as health hazards that the laid-back tea leaf can only dream of. In other words, coffee is macho. It logs in slightly below blowfish and a little above football on the Pain-Indexed Virility Scale. Madison Avenue knows this, at one point hiring guy-icon Joe DiMaggio to sell coffeemakers.

Thanks to advertising, the genderization of tea is firmly entrenched in our culture. A television commercial for bottled tea ran in heavy rotation a few summers back. The tea ads captured my attention because they featured a shouting male voice-over, the sort of voice you usually hear over your car radio, bellowing, "Sixty-four MONSTER TRUCKS!!! Meet Playboy's MISS AUGUST!!! BE THERE!!!" The tea-slamming rebels in the ad, however, were three superfeminine supermodels. "This ain't no SIPPIN' TEA!!!" the voice sneered, implying that being gulped is all the envelope-pushing that tea can stand.

I don't get it. Time was, men were men, and men drank tea (when they weren't launching it into the bay, that is). The mountain men of the Hudson's Bay and Northwest Companies so desperately relied on tea that they actually seeded the West with the Labrador tea plant, whose leaves they used to stretch or replace dwindling stores of black tea. Rugged outdoorsmen, known to go a year between trips to town, collapsed in a quivering mass of jelly if a tea bog were more than a day's schlep away. And hold on to your boxers, brothers: when we say Labrador, we're not just talking tea, but *herb* tea. It wasn't only mountain men sipping non-tea plants; macho city patriots, unable to stomach supporting the British East India Company, turned to steeping common garden or wild plants so they could thumb their noses at the enemy.

Of course, men used to wear wigs and face powder too, habits generally frowned on in the weight rooms of today. But I'd still argue that for the man of action, tea—herb or otherwise—beats the combat boots off coffee. All you need is reasonably tasty organic matter and boiling water. No fuss, no gizmos. Yet somehow, somewhere, between Lewis and Clark and the Civil War, American guys stepped off the tea wagon and we've been chumps ever since. Yankee and Rebel soldiers packed clanking coffee pots in their marching kits, brewed the stuff over tiny campfires and waited, feet freezing in the snow, while it took its sweet time perking up. Ditto the cowboys, who had to plop a raw egg in their noxious brew to strain it. American soldiers in this century dipped barely-drinkable boiled coffee from a huge cauldron; the last GIs in line got half a cup of grounds. These days, commandos fall back on foil packets of "instant coffee-type beverage, hot." This is progress?

I don't think so. Tea has the advantage of extreme portability. Given a fistful of decent leaves and a heat source, a guy can brew the same cup of Darjeeling or peppermint tea at base camp on Mount Everest—before he succumbs to hypothermia— that he enjoys in his kitchen at home. Logic, however, is probably beside the point of the tea-coffee controversy. This is ultimately an emotional issue, turning less on what men do than how they feel about it. Given that the words "I feel" are more threatening than a flowered tea cozy to some men, it may be a while before most American males rediscover tea.

I was lucky. My own British roots bred in me a certain "tea sense," a Pavlovian reaction to the aromatic khaki swirl that science has yet to investigate. As long as tea is on, I'm all right. You say my girlfriend just ran off with my CD collection? I fire up the kettle. Have I slogged ten miles in mud and freezing rain, and got ten more to go? My hiking stove heats a quart of water in two minutes. My agent called to say she could sell my manuscript on jet-ski maintenance, if only it had a sex scene? A splash of hot water and a spot of milk restore equilibrium to an unpredictable world.

The re-hinging power of tea is real, and real men respect it. A retired U.S. Army officer whom I once interviewed remembered seeing Royal Air Force pilots blast enemy fighters out of the North African sky for hours on end. At the first lull, the Brits would land their Spitfires abruptly, leap onto the sand, and pour a hasty cup of strong tea. Forty years later, the American still remembered how the twentysomething flyers called each other "old man" and chatted like businessmen on an evening train. But not for long. Soon, yet another squadron of Messerschmitts would come snarling low over the dunes. Exhausted, grimy, and hungry, the RAF men dumped the lees of their cuppas in the dust and, with a quiet "Tally ho," roared off to defy death again.

Coffee achievers, indeed.

Energizing Teas

Western society has a love-hate relationship with its own frenzied pace. We lament what stress has done to our lives, yet we're always finding ways to further complicate them. We decry chaos while we deliberately multiply it.

The simplicity of tea refreshes and reaffirms. After all, you cannot speed up the making of tea; it only takes a few minutes as it is. Tea can be soothing while still providing a bit of the same energy boost as coffee. Black tea contains about half the caffeine of coffee; green tea contains only one sixth to one eighth as much. The amount in any given cup varies with brewing methods and length of steeping. Tea bags produce a cup with more caffeine; quickly brewed loose tea has less.

Even the small amount of caffeine in tea can create problems for some people; its stimulating effect can be accompanied by jitters and difficulty concentrating. Most of the teas in this chapter are caffeine-free. Instead, they use herbs long thought to boost energy—Siberian ginseng, for one. They also employ the cool, clean, invigorating flavor of citrus elements or the warming effects of spices such as cinnamon and ginger. Some include immune-system stimulants that help the body protect or repair itself. One offers tea drinkers a stealthy way to fit into the coffee culture. If caffeine doesn't bother you, add black or green tea to the tea-less recipes for a more potent pick-me-up.

To choose an energizing tea, take an olfactory tour of your health food store's bulk section. Close your eyes and take a whiff of the ingredients in teas you're considering making. Which ones are you drawn to? Which ones seem to perk you up after a long day? While the smell and taste of some herbs differ distinctly, the ones whose scents strongly attract you will usually be pleasing in a cup.

> **Herb teas employ Siberian ginseng, citrus elements, or warming spices to achieve an invigorating effect.**

Athlete's Tea

Brigitte Mars

In this tea, Brigitte combines Siberian ginseng for energy, ginger for better digestion and spicy flavor, hawthorn leaf and flower to boost circulation, and a Chinese herb, he shou wu root, to help you run, bicycle, swim, or climb that extra mile. The licorice and ginger also help make it taste good.

To blend 48 servings

1/4 cup plus 2 tablespoons *Siberian ginseng root (also known as eleuthero)*
1/4 cup plus 2 tablespoons *licorice root*
1/4 cup plus 2 tablespoons *dried, chopped ginger root*
1/4 cup plus 2 tablespoons *he shou wu root (this herb is also known as fo-ti; its Latin name is* Polygonum multiflorum)
1/4 cup plus 2 tablespoons *hawthorn leaves and flowers*

Combine ingredients in a 2-cup container. Store away from light up to one year.

To brew 1 large cup

2 teaspoons blend
1½ cups water

Add blend and water to a French coffee press or large mug with a cover; steep for 15 minutes.

Stealth Iced Latté

Robert R. Henderson

This refreshing version of iced tea is almost easier than a trip to the coffeehouse. Robert relies on its caffeine kick and latté-like look to preserve his secret identity as the only non-coffee drinker in the Pacific Northwest.

To brew one tall cold glass

*1 teaspoon or 1 tea bag strong black tea, such
   as Assam or English Breakfast
3 ice cubes
1/2 cup whipping cream
1/2 teaspoon sugar
1 to 1½ cups water*

Whip the cream until it forms soft peaks; add 1/2 teaspoon sugar, or to taste, and refrigerate. Steep tea in just-boiled water for 3 to 5 minutes, then chill. Coarsely crush ice cubes in a blender. Add tea (strain first if using loose leaves) to blender; blend until just mixed. Add whipped cream and whirl until tea is foamy. Serve in a tall glass. If you want to complete the latté disguise, sprinkle a little ground cinnamon or nutmeg on top.

Focus and Remember Tea

Caroline MacDougall

*T*his tea combines citrus flavors to perk up the senses, ginkgo and gotu kola to foster clear thinking, and rosemary and lavender for their fresh, clean scents. Stevia adds sweetness without calories. If you like your tea a bit sweeter, increase the amount of stevia slightly, but remember that a little of this herb goes a long way.

To blend 55 servings

1 cup crumbled lemon balm leaves
1/4 cup orange peel
1/2 cup gotu kola herb
1/3 cup ginkgo leaves
2 tablespoons rosemary
1 tablespoon lavender flowers
1 tablespoon stevia herb
1 tablespoon sweet orange oil

Combine ingredients in a glass jar. Add the orange oil. Shake well to blend and distribute the oil. Store away from light for up to a year.

To brew 1 large cup

2 teaspoons blend
1½ cups water

Steep blend for 4 to 5 minutes in just-boiled water. Strain if needed.

Stressful Situation Tea

Caroline MacDougall

*n*aturally sweetened with vanilla and licorice, this tea combines the balancing influences of peppermint and the calming, mood-lifting effect of kava-kava. Siberian ginseng boosts energy, and astragalus and schisandra stimulate the immune system.

To blend 55 servings

*1/2 cup Siberian ginseng root (also known
  as eleuthero)*
1/4 cup licorice root
1 cup peppermint leaves
1/3 cup kava-kava root
1/3 cup dried orange peel
1/2 cup astragalus root
2 tablespoons whole schisandra berries
2 tablespoons vanilla extract

Combine all ingredients a large bowl. Stir well to distribute the extract. Store in a glass jar away from light for up to a year.

To brew 1 large cup

1½ cups water
2 teaspoons blend

Steep blend in just-boiled water for 4 to 5 minutes. Strain; drink warm.

Brainstorming Tea

Brigitte Mars

The herbs in this tea are used in larger doses to help enhance blood and oxygen flow to the brain; the spices stimulate the senses. Brigitte designed it for sharing with a friend while cranking out new ideas or collaborating on a project.

To blend 30 servings

1/4 cup aniseed
1/4 cup ginkgo leaves
1/4 cup coarsely crushed cinnamon sticks
1/4 cup coarsely crushed cloves
1/4 cup Siberian ginseng root (eleuthero)

Combine ingredients. Store away from light for up to a year.

To brew 2 cups

2 heaping teaspoons blend
2 cups water

Bring water just to a boil; add blend and water to a French coffee press or a warmed teapot. Steep for 15 minutes; strain before serving if necessary.

Oh-Too-Early Wake-Up Tea

Susan Wittig Albert

*H*ave trouble finding your brain in the morning? Susan blended the fresh, clean taste and scent of rosemary with green tea for kick and then added some familiar morning flavors, including cinnamon and citrus.

To blend 30 servings

1/2 cup green tea
1/4 cup rosemary
1/4 cup rosehips
1/4 cup dried lemon or orange peel
3 tablespoons cloves, coarsely crushed
3-inch piece of cinnamon stick, crushed

Combine ingredients in a glass jar. Store away from light for up to a year.

To brew 1 large cup

1 heaping teaspoon blend
1½ cups water

Heat water to a simmer. Combine water and blend in a large mug; cover and steep for 5 to 10 minutes.

Relaxing Teas

*L*ike music, tea can soothe the savage mind. Lucky for us savages, many herbs that assist relaxation, calm anxiety, and foster smooth sleep also taste good in tea.

Take chamomile, for example. According to some sources, it has been used for digestive problems since the first century A.D. The ancient Greeks called it "ground apple" for its pleasing scent. Maude Grieve's *A Modern Herbal*, published in 1931, touts it as an "old-fashioned but extremely efficacious remedy for hysterical and nervous affections in women, " citing its "wonderfully soothing, sedative and absolutely harmless effect." Herbalists have long recommended it for colic, indigestion, insomnia, menstrual cramps, and aching muscles.

The sweet scent of crushed lemon balm leaves, meanwhile, is considered cooling and calming, a tension reliever that helps improve the mood. Like chamomile, lemon balm was known to both the Greeks and medieval European herbalists; Gerard wrote in his *Herbal* that it "comforteth the hart and driveth away all sadnesse." Also like

chamomile, it helps ease indigestion. Peppermint, meanwhile, is probably one of the best-known and most-used tea herbs of all time. Dried leaves were found in Egyptian pyramids dating from 1000 B.C. In calming teas, peppermint adds a sweet flavor and additional digestive benefits. Catnip is another stomach settler with an intriguing history. An Irish herbalist wrote of it in 1735: "Drunk with salt and honey, it expels worms from the body." Other old herbals recommend catnip for complaints ranging from nightmares to dandruff. Passionflower, on the other hand, is a relative newcomer, first mentioned in herbals around 1898. Sedative and antispasmodic, passionflower is used in medicinal chewing gum in Europe.

Relaxation doesn't always mean taking a snooze, however. If tension is a problem, but retaining or restoring alertness is desired, the herbal teas in this chapter can be blended with black or green tea. One recipe, a green tea spiced with anise, cloves, and licorice, is designed to go with leisure reading. Another includes basil and thyme, to help restore the appetite by recalling savory foods.

Banish Exhaustion Tea

Sheron Buehele

This is a tea for days when you've played too many roles—parent, child, employee, boss, sympathetic sibling, responsible pet owner. It's also for those nights when you're exhausted, yet sleep eludes you. Peppermint, basil, and thyme give this tea a strong flavor, but also one that helps to soothe and relax. Sheron reaches for this tea at the first sign of a chest cold.

To blend 36 servings

1/2 cup peppermint leaves
1/4 cup basil leaves
2 tablespoons thyme

Mix herbs thoroughly in a glass jar. Store away from light for up to a year.

To brew 1 cup

1 teaspoon blend
1 cup water
Honey to taste

Steep blend for no more than 4 minutes in just-boiled water (the tea becomes too strong if steeped longer). Serve hot or cold with honey.

Kicked-Back Evening Tea

Portia Meares

C elebrate glorious simplicity with this easy tea—herbs that are easy to grow, easy to blend, and easy to drink. Portia says that the flavor of her home-grown dried chamomile flowers is far superior to that of chamomile you can buy (for herb drying instructions, see pages 10–11.) This is a lovely tea for the end of a long, productive day.

To blend 32 servings

1/2 cup chamomile flowers
1/2 cup lemon balm leaves

Combine the herbs in a glass container. Store away from light for up to a year.

To brew 1 cup

1 heaping teaspoon blend
1 cup water

Steep blend for 5 minutes in just-boiled water. Strain if necessary.

Sweet Dreams Tea

Maggie Oster

This tea combines lemon balm, a sedative and stomach soother, with passionflower, an herb commonly taken to help relieve nervous tension and muscle spasms. Catnip stimulates cats, but has a reputation for calming people.

To blend 32 servings

1 cup lemon balm leaves
1/3 cup passionflower herb
2/3 cup catnip leaves

Combine the herbs in a glass container. Store away from light for up to a year.

To brew 1 cup

1 tablespoon blend
1 to 1½ cup water

Add just-boiled water and tea blend to a cup, mug, or small teapot; steep for 10 minutes. Strain and serve.

Kiss and Make Up Tea

Brigitte Mars

*Y*ou say tomato, he says tomahto. Don't call the whole thing off. Retreat to your separate corners with a tea that Brigitte formulated to calm frayed nerves and foster feelings of harmony and peace. Practitioners of Traditional Chinese Medicine believe that the liver is the seat of anger, and that dandelion root helps to cleanse that organ, while jujube date is thought to soothe the spirit and relieve moodiness. Western herbalists use chamomile and skullcap as calming herbs. Meanwhile, licorice root helps sweeten the cup.

To blend 64 servings

1/2 cup dried chamomile flowers
1/4 cup licorice root
1/2 cup dandelion root
1/2 cup skullcap herb
1/4 cup jujube dates

Mix ingredients thoroughly. Store away from light for up to a year.

To brew 2 cups

2 heaping teaspoons of blend
2 cups water

Put herbs into a French coffee press or warmed teapot; add just-boiled water and steep for 15 minutes. Strain if needed.

Curl Up With a Good Book Tea

Susan Wittig Albert

Susan, author of the China Bayles mystery series, gardens and writes in Bertram, Texas. She likes this tea because the chamomile is calming, while the small amount of caffeine in the green tea fosters alertness, so you don't wind up nodding over the pages. Hibiscus adds vitamin C, tartness, and a bright color.

To blend 40 servings

1/4 cup green tea
1/4 cup dried chamomile flowers
1/4 cup dried hibiscus flowers
3 tablespoons licorice root
1 tablespoon dried orange peel
1 tablespoon cloves
1 tablespoon aniseed
3 to 4 vanilla beans, finely chopped and dried

Coarsely crush the cloves in a mortar and pestle. Mix ingredients thoroughly in a glass jar. Store away from light for up to a year.

To brew 2 cups

2 heaping teaspoons blend
2 cups water

Add just-boiled water and blend to a warmed teapot. Steep for 5 minutes or longer, depending on desired strength.

Soothing Catnip Tea
Pat Dice

Stevia is an alternative sweetener that doesn't affect blood-sugar metabolism. That makes it ideal for diabetics and others who shouldn't use sugar or merely wish to avoid it. Pat recommends this tea to help ease restlessness and tension. Tangerine peel gives it a touch of citrus zing.

To blend 48 servings

3/4 cup catnip leaves
1/2 cup skullcap herb
1/4 cup spearmint leaves
1 tablespoon dried tangerine peel
1- to 2-inch piece of cinnamon stick, crushed
1 teaspoon stevia

Mix ingredients in a glass container. Store away from light for up to a year.

To brew 1 cup

1½ teaspoons blend
1 cup water

Steep the blend for 3 to 5 minutes in just-boiled water. Strain and drink before bedtime.

Seasonal Teas

Spicy and warming for winter, iced with fresh ingredients in summer, tea adapts to any climate. Teas for winter often rely on spices such as cinnamon, cloves, ginger, and star anise. Teas that use these ingredients combine well with hot apple cider or wine.

Cardamom, a spice common in Scandinavian and Indian cooking, appears in several teas in this chapter. Native to India and Sri Lanka, it has been used as a spice, a medicine, and a perfume for thousands of years. The plant's yellow-green seed pods contain about 20 dark brown seeds. Recipes that use cardamom will specify either the whole seed pods or the seeds. Sometimes the seeds should be crushed or bruised before using them in tea. Cardamom has historically been used in digestive remedies, so in addition to smelling wonderful, teas containing cardamom go well with rich holiday foods.

Teas for spring celebrate the reawakening of the garden and wild land around you. For example, one tea in this chapter combines leaves of stinging nettle with fresh spearmint and rose petals. The young, spring shoots and leaves of the nettle plant, *Urtica dioica*, have long been used as a spring cleanser that is rich in minerals. Nettles can be found growing wild, or tame and dried in the aisles of your health food store.

Finally, summer teas take advantage of an abundance of fresh herbs and fruits. Try making your favorite tea as a sun tea with lemon wedges, berries, or fresh mint as a garnish. If lemons are a bargain, squeeze a dozen or so into ice cube trays and freeze their juice to enjoy throughout the hot days. If your mint takes over the garden, fresh mint tea is a way to put handfuls to good use; it's also a wonderful closer to a hearty meal from the grill.

Teas for fall and winter are spiced to stand up to hearty harvest meals; teas for spring and summer celebrate the reawakening of the land.

Fruits of the Fall Tea

Caroline MacDougall

*T*his spicy, tangy, highly fragrant tea goes well with autumn foods. Rooibos is a South African herb that is caffeine free.

To blend 60 servings

1/3 cup dried apple pieces, chopped in small pieces
1/4 cup hibiscus flowers
1/4 cup rooibos or black tea
1/4 cup rose hip shells
1/4 cup allspice berries
1/3 cup wintergreen leaves
1 tablepoon currants
15 inches of cinnamon stick
  or 1/4 cup ground cinnamon
1 rounded tablespoon birch bark
1 teaspoon wintergreen essential oil

Combine dry ingredients in a glass jar. Add the wintergreen oil; shake well to blend and distribute it. Store away from light for up to a year.

To brew 4 cups

4 heaping teaspoons blend
4 cups water
Honey if desired

Add just-boiled water and blend to a warmed teapot. Steep 4 to 5 minutes. Sweeten with honey; serve hot.

Pre-Ski Tea

Elizabeth Bergstrom

The warming flavor of cardamom in this tea is a nod to Elizabeth's Scandinavian heritage. She finds it a perfect brew for a cold, crisp winter morning, just before hitting the slopes.

To blend 48 servings

1/2 cup peppermint leaves
1/4 cup black tea
1/4 cup coarsely ground cinnamon stick
1½ teaspoon cardamom seeds, outer pods removed
1½ teaspoon coarsely ground star anise
1 teaspoon coarsely ground cloves

Grind the cardamom, star anise and cloves in a mortar and pestle in small batches before measuring. Combine with the remaining ingredients; mix well and store away from light for up to a year.

To brew 1 cup

1½ teaspoons blend
1 cup water
Milk and honey to taste

Add blend to just-boiled water; steep for 5 minutes. Strain if needed; add milk and honey if desired.

Warming Winter Tea

Brigitte Mars

This recipe is among Brigitte's favorites. Its ingredients are common to many spiced teas, but it replaces black tea with dandelion root—a good cleansing herb for a season filled with rich food and drink. Served with milk, honey and a dash of nutmeg, this tea can be a low-calorie stand-in for eggnog. To roast dandelion root, see page 14.

To blend 48 servings

1 cup roasted dandelion root
1/4 teaspoon coarsely crushed cinnamon
1/4 cup cardamom seeds, outer pod removed
1/4 cup dried, chopped ginger root
1/4 cup star anise

Coarsely crush the cinnamon, cardamom and star anise with a mortar and pestle. Store away from light for up to a year.

To brew 4 cups

6 teaspoons blend
4 teaspoons honey
4 cups water
Milk and nutmeg to taste

Add blend to just-boiled water; cover the saucepan and simmer for about 10 minutes. Strain the liquid into mugs. Add 1 teaspoon of honey and a splash of milk to each mug. Garnish with a sprinkle of nutmeg.

Evergreen Tea

Robert R. Henderson

Resinous evergreen aromas mingle with peppermint in this strong, fragrant winter tea. Robert's philosophy is to buy nothing that he can wildcraft, so he picks and roasts his own juniper berries for this tea. Berries from Rocky Mountain or Utah juniper species will work, but so will purchased berries. Juniper infusions can be a kidney irritant for some people, so this tea is best as a holiday treat, not a daily drink.

To roast juniper berries

1/3 cup juniper berries

Preheat oven to 300 degrees. Put berries in a glass pan or on a cookie sheet and roast until they are dark brown, crisp, and smoking. Let cool; grind with a mortar and pestle. Yields about 2 tablespoons.

To brew 4 cups

2 tablespoons ground roasted juniper berries
2 tablespoons cinnamon stick, coarsely crushed
2 slices fresh ginger root
5 whole cloves
1/2 teaspoon ground nutmeg
1 8-inch candy cane, broken up
4 cups water

Crush the cloves in a mortar and pestle. Bring water to a boil. Add all ingredients to pot; cover and steep for 5 to 10 minutes and strain. Serve with milk or cream.

Winter Sunshine Tea

Sharon Lovejoy

With its blend of citrus and spices, this tea smells wonderful just bubbling on the stove, which it needs to do for longer than most teas. Use the whole, unshelled cardamom pods and whole vanilla bean; the extra simmering time slowly releases their scents and flavors.

To brew 6 cups

3½ tablespoons freshly grated ginger root
1½ tablespoons lemon zest
1½ tablespoons orange zest
9 cardamom pods
8 cups water
6 cinnamon sticks for garnish
A 2-inch piece of vanilla bean
Honey to taste

Combine all ingredients except the honey in a non-reactive saucepan. Bring to a rolling boil, then simmer uncovered for 20 to 25 minutes. Pour through a strainer and into a warmed teapot. Serve in cups with a cinnamon stick; add honey to taste.

Thank Heaven It's Spring Tea

Brigitte Mars

rigitte developed this tea for *The Herb Companion* to celebrate National Herb Week, the first week of May each year. It employs nettle leaves, which not only cleanse the system but contain iron to boost energy for spring chores and sports. The other herbs celebrate the season's new colors and tastes.

To brew 4 cups

2 heaping teaspoons chopped fresh nettle leaves, or 1 heaping teaspoon dried
2 heaping teaspoons chopped fresh spearmint leaves, or 1 heaping teaspoon dried
2 teaspoons unsprayed fresh rose petals, white heels removed, or 1 teaspoon dried
1/2 teaspoon dried aniseed, slightly crushed
4 fresh strawberries, sliced
1 quart water

Bring the water to a boil. Place the remaining ingredients into a warmed teapot. Pour boiling water over the herbs and strawberries, cover, and let steep for 10 minutes. Strain and serve. To make as a sun tea, put the herbs in a glass jar, pour room-temperature or cold water over them, then set the jar outside in the sun and forget about it for an hour or two. Serve over ice with fresh strawberries as a garnish.

Apple-Mint Iced Tea

Audrey Seano

Audrey, assistant editor of *The Herb Companion*, concocted this tea and the next two fruity iced drinks for a recent issue. They combine fresh herbs, tea and fruit, so they're great for knocking the dust out of your throat. Audrey uses unsweetened apple juice to make the tea below; if you use sweetened apple juice, omit the honey.

To brew 4 10-ounce glasses

1 quart water
6 teaspoons black tea or 6 regular tea bags
1 cup fresh peppermint leaves
2 tablespoons honey
2 cups apple juice
Fresh mint sprigs and apple slices (optional)

Combine black tea or tea bags, peppermint leaves, and just-boiled water in teapot and steep for 5 to 10 minutes. Strain, stir in honey and chill. To serve, combine with apple juice. Pour over ice and garnish with mint sprigs—the fuzzy leaves of apple mint add texture—and apple slices. (To keep apple slices from browning, sprinkle with a little fresh lemon juice.)

Lemon-Hibiscus Iced Tea

Audrey Seano

A touch of sassy citrus flavor and a crimson color make this tea a favorite of children and a festive party beverage. Hibiscus is also high in Vitamin C.

To brew 12 cups or 8 12-ounce glasses

2 quarts water
1/4 cup dried jasmine flowers
1 cup dried hibiscus flowers
4 cups lemonade, preferably fresh or
   reconstituted from frozen concentrate
8 lemon slices for garnish

Pour boiling water over the flowers. Steep for 5 to 10 minutes. Strain and chill. Add cold lemonade. Serve over ice; garnish with lemon slices.

Fresh and Fruity Iced Tea

Audrey Seano

Pineapple sage is a bushy, tender species with a delicious, fruity aroma. It sprouts bright red flowers in the late summer and fall. Its leaves give this tea a subtle, delicate flavor.

To brew 2 quarts
or 6 10-ounce glasses

2 quarts water
1/2 cup fresh pineapple sage leaves
1/4 cup dried chamomile flowers
1/4 cup dried rose hips
1/4 cup chopped fresh lemon zest
Fresh pineapple sage leaves and blossoms
*   for garnish*

Bring water to a boil. Add herbs and lemon zest; cover and steep for 5 to 10 minutes. Strain and chill. Pour over ice; garnish with fresh pineapple sage leaves or blossoms.

Six-Lemon Summer Triumph Tea

Portia Meares

This is a gardener's tea, made from fresh herbs and designed for sipping on the porch after a day of battles with bugs, weeds, drought, or floods. You may substitute 1/2 teaspoon dried lemon grass if the fresh herb is unavailable. This tea uses the leaves of a particular variety of a plant widely known as a scented geraniums; they are actually pelargoniums, a different species. These leaves may be omitted, or you can substitute another variety. Portia sometimes adds a cup of unsweetened Summer Triumph to a gallon of regular sun tea for a less-caffeinated, lemony drink.

To brew 4 cups

1 teaspoon fresh lemon-scented thyme leaves
1 teaspoon fresh lemon basil leaves
1 teaspoon fresh lemon balm leaves
1 teaspoon fresh lemon grass (use lower parts of the
    leaves)
1 teaspoon fresh lemon verbena leaves
1 teaspoon fresh Mabel Grey scented pelargonium leaves
4 cups water
Honey or sugar if desired

Bring 4 cups water just to a boil. Add herbs and just-boiled water to a warmed teapot. Steep for 5 to 8 minutes. Strain and serve with honey or sugar.

Festive Teas

Any tea can be festive—just add food, friends, and a reason to celebrate. You can go to the elaborate excesses of the British high tea, with side tables for each guest and separate courses of savory and sweet foods in tiny portions. Or you can create a simpler tea party with a buffet of seasonal dishes. You can build an entire meal based on foods that use tea and herb tea as ingredients, such as tea eggs, which are hard-boiled eggs that are gently cracked, then simmered again in tea and spices. There are many cookbooks devoted to dishes that gracefully accompany tea. The only limit is imagination and the size of your gathering site.

Festive teas can be an opportunity to show off a collection of teapots or unusual cups and mugs. To serve tea to a crowd, it can be brewed, then kept warm, in an electric urn. Such urns that have long been used for coffee, however, may give the tea a muddy taste, so if you plan to use one for a large party, give it a trial run first. A soak with half distilled vinegar and half water may help to remove any flavors that have permeated the container.

The teas in this chapter were developed to acccompany specific foods or occasions. Moroccan Mint Tea complements the complex spices and rich tastes of Middle Eastern food. Company Brunch Tea is a custom-blended breakfast tea, designed for holiday gatherings. Lover's Tea and Private Conversation Tea, on the other hand, were made to be savored and shared *a deux*. I Believe I'll Have Another Cookie Tea brews just one cup, to go with those solitary double-chocolate-chip-macadamia-nut celebrations. And Overindulger's Tea is based on herbs that help gently cleanse the body of the aftereffects of too-vigorous celebrating.

> The only limit to celebrations centered on tea is your imagination and the size of your patio, garden, parlor, or living room.

I Believe I'll Have Another Cookie Tea

Brigitte Mars

"Everyone has to believe in something. . ." begins the saying that inspired this tea. Its warm and spicy herbs enhance digestion, and the fennel is naturally sweet and tasty.

To blend 54 servings

1/4 cup coarsely crushed cinnamon stick
1/4 cup chopped, dried ginger root
1/4 cup fennel seed
1/4 cup cardamom seed
1/8 cup peppermint leaves

Mix ingredients in a glass container. Store away from light for up to a year.

To brew 1 cup

1½ teaspoons blend
1½ cup water

Add blend and just-boiled water to a French coffee press or warmed teapot for 15 minutes. Strain if needed; add milk if desired. Dunk cookies and drink warm.

Splendid Woman's Tea

Sheron Buchele

Sheron conceived of this tea while teaching a class on the healing uses of culinary herbs. She wanted a tea that used common kitchen herbs, but was also delicious. Sage and peppermint teas are high in minerals that women often lack in their diets, such as iron, magnesium, and calcium. Herbalists consider peppermint a balancing herb—one that fosters alertness when you are sleepy, but calms jangled nerves.

To blend 60 servings

1 cup peppermint leaves
1/2 cup lemon verbena leaves
1/4 cup whole sage leaves
1/4 cup rose petals

Put the ingredients into a mixing bowl; crumble the leaves coarsely. Mix ingredients thoroughly; store in a glass container away from light for no more than a year.

To brew 4 cups

5 heaping teaspoons blend
4 cups water
Honey to taste

Add blend and 4 cups just-boiled water to a warmed teapot. Steep for no more than 4 minutes. Strain and serve with honey if desired; drink hot or cold.

Orange-Bergamot Tea

Susan Belsinger

*E*arl Grey tea gets its wonderful scent and flavor from the oil of *Citrus bergamia*, the bergamot orange. Two common herbs mimic its aroma and taste: *Monarda didyma*, commonly known as bergamot or bee balm, and *Mentha aquatica* 'Citrata,' known as orange or bergamot mint. Combined, they give this tea the intensity of its namesake without the caffeine. This is a tea that works with either fresh or dried herbs; directions for both are given below.

To blend 12 servings

2/3 cup dried bee balm leaves
2/3 cup dried orange mint leaves
About 2/3 cup dried flowers of bee balm
* and/or orange mint*

Combine herbs in a glass container. Store away from light for up to a year

To brew 4 cups

2/3 cup dried herb blend
OR:
1/2 cup fresh bee balm leaves
1/2 cup fresh bee balm flowers
1 cup orange mint leaves and/or flowers
PLUS:
Orange blossom or other mild-flavored honey
Orange mint sprigs or flowers for garnish
4 cups water

Add the fresh or dried herbs and just-boiled water to a warmed teapot. Steep fresh herbs for 10 minutes, dried for 5 minutes. Strain, sweeten if desired and serve.

Company Brunch Tea
Art Tucker

This tea gives a citrus twist and a little spice to a familiar breakfast taste. It also complements breakfast foods and meats nicely.

To blend 36 servings

1 cup orange pekoe-type tea
1 tablespoon dried tangerine peel
1½ teaspoons freshly ground allspice
1½ teaspoons chopped cinnamon stick
1½ teaspoons coarsely ground cloves
1½ teaspoons coarsely crumbled lemon balm, lemon grass, or lemon verbena leaves

Mix well and store for up to a year.

To brew 8 cups

2 quarts water
4 tablespoons blend
Milk, honey, or sugar to taste

Heat water just to a boil in a non-reactive pan. Add loose tea; steep for no more than 5 minutes. Strain into a thermal carafe or large urn.

Lover's Tea

Pat Dice

Experts say that the sexiest part of the body is the brain. This tea contains ginkgo leaf, which in larger doses helps boost circulation to that vital organ. The lavender and spices smell good, and ginger warms the metabolism. Damiana has long been considered an aphrodisiac, though little research has been done on it. However, damiana tea should not be drunk by pregnant women.

To blend 36 servings

1/2 cup ginkgo leaves
1/2 cup white Chinese ginseng root
1/4 cup dried ginger root
1/8 cup damiana leaves
1/8 cup lavender flowers
2 tablespoons chopped dried orange peel
1 tablespoon cardamom seed
1 teaspoon whole cloves
1- to 2-inch piece of cinnamon stick

Crush the cardamom seed, clove, and cinnamon in a mortar and pestle. Blend with the herbs and store away from light for up to a year.

To brew 2 cups:

4 teaspoons blend
2 cups water

Add blend to just-boiled water; cover and let steep 6 to 8 minutes. Strain and drink warm.

Overindulger's Tea

Maggie Oster

Maggie designed this tea to be drunk both before and after big celebrations, or by people who can't seem to avoid hangovers no matter how prudently they imbibe. Dandelion root is a gently cleansing tonic for the liver. Ginger may help to ease the nausea of a morning after. Hibiscus adds color, flavor, and Vitamin C.

To blend 14 servings

1 cup hibiscus flowers
1/2 cup dandelion root
1/4 cup finely chopped crystallized ginger

Combine ingredients in a glass container. Store away from light for up to a year

To brew 1 cup

2 tablespoons blend
1 cup water
1 teaspoon honey

Add blend and water to a saucepan. Bring to a boil, then reduce heat and simmer for 20 minutes. Strain and serve.

Private Conversation Tea

Susan Clotfelter

A tea purist would never adulterate a fine Darjeeling with anything other than sugar or honey. This blend is a way to help out a Darjeeling that has failed to meet expectations, or one that has sat too long on the tea shelf. Gotu kola is used medicinally to assist memory and ease rheumatism; here it contributes earthy and grassy notes. Orange peel adds sweetness, while a touch of cloves and cardamom add subtle bite and fragrance.

To blend 48 servings

1 cup Darjeeling (or other mild black tea)
1/2 cup gotu kola herb
5 tablespoons dried orange peel, broken into small (pea-sized) pieces
3 tablespoons cardamom seeds, bruised in a mortar and pestle
2 teaspoons coarsely crushed whole cloves

Combine all ingredients in a glass container. Store away from light for up to a year.

To brew 2 cups

4 teaspoons blend
2½ cups water
honey or sugar to taste

Combine tea blend and just-boiled water in a warmed teapot or French coffee press. Steep for 3 to 4 minutes (Darjeeling is one of those black teas that goes bitter quickly). Add honey or sugar to taste.

Moroccan Mint Tea

Susan Belsinger

This tea is often served at the close of meals in Morocco, but it goes well after any long, rich repast of Mediterranean origin. To be a traditional Moroccan tea, the tea must be mild green tea, and the mint must be fresh spearmint (absolutely not dried). Susan says it is traditionally served very sweet; sugar always remains in the bottom of the glasses in Morocco. This recipe originally appeared in *Herbs in the Kitchen*, which she wrote with Carolyn Dille.

To brew 6 small glasses

1 heaping tablespoon mild green tea, such as
   Dragonwell or gunpowder
About 2 loosely packed cups of spearmint
   leaves
1/4 to 1/2 cup sugar
4 to 5 cups boiling water
Fresh mint sprigs for garnish

Add the green tea to a large, warmed teapot, then add the fresh spearmint and the sugar. Fill the pot with boiling water. Steep for 5 minutes. Pour into small glasses, adding a fresh mint sprig to each glass.

Green Teas

To drink green tea is to reach back in time, to pluck a thread of history that unites Chinese legend, twelfth-century Buddhist ritual, arduous trade routes, and a long tradition of painstaking cultivation and production by hand. To drink green tea is also to partake of one of the most intriguing subjects of current medical research.

Brewed from the minimally processed leaves of the *Camellia sinensis* plant, green tea is now being studied for its antioxidant qualities and its potential to prevent cancer. The research is, in most cases, very promising; green tea appears to help prevent rectal, colon, pancreatic, and skin cancers. It also seems to have the same ability to help prevent heart disease as some other antioxidants, and has some antibacterial and antimicrobial action. Its constituents may even help defend against acne and tooth decay.

Green tea was the first tea; the oxidation process that produces oolong and black tea was introduced in the fourteenth century as a way to preserve loose tea. Green tea has about a fourth as much caffeine as black tea, although still enough (about six to thirty milligrams per cup) to boost alertness in some people. As with black tea, leaves of green tea that are chopped into tiny pieces to fit into tea bags release more caffeine than whole leaves; so does a longer brewing time. Green tea differs from black tea in significant ways. The flavor is subtle, mild, a little grassy; the color is usually pale greenish-gold. Tea experts say that the water used to brew green tea should be between 170 and 185 degrees Fahrenheit, not boiling; a gentle simmer is plenty hot. To make your green tea stronger, either steep it longer or add more tea, but don't use hotter water. Green tea also is traditionally drunk warm, not steaming hot.

There are several types of green tea. Some processing methods produce what's known as gunpowder tea, which is green tea rolled into round pellets that unfold when steeped. Another type, *genmaicha*, combines green tea leaves with fire-roasted rice, lending a slightly salty, smoky flavor to the tea. Some tea recipes call for Dragonwell green tea; this is China's most popular variety.

Matcha, or powdered green tea, is the type used in the Japanese tea ceremony. The tea and hot water are stirred together with a bamboo whisk, creating a frothy emerald brew. The ceremony is carefully orchestrated to provide a respite from the cares of everyday life and restore tranquility; numerous schools in

Japan and a few in other countries offer instruction in conducting the ceremony. You can study this ancient ritual, or devise your own, focusing on tea and herbs of high quality, a serene and beautiful setting, implements whose craftsmanship pleases you, and guests who can willingly leave the outside world behind.

Some tea connoisseurs urge using a separate pot solely for green tea, so that its flavor does not become tainted with the strong tastes of black tea. Whether or not you need to do this may depend on how porous your teapot is. A well-cleaned glass teapot may never acquire built-up flavors. However, if you have the luck to own a Yixing teapot—a type of reddish brown, unglazed Chinese stoneware—you may want to use it only for one type of tea.

Like any other tea, green tea can be easily blended with leaves and flowers of other herbs for additional flavors, aromas, and health benefits. If you wish to blend woody parts of herbs, such as roots, barks, or berries, with green tea, you may need to simmer them separately to unlock their flavors and benefits. Lemon-scented herbs and bright, astringent herbs such as rosemary, hibiscus, lemon verbena, and lemon balm work wonderfully with green tea. Heavier spices may overpower its delicate flavor. By all means, sample the increasing variety of commercially-blended green teas available in tea bags today. But you should also experience green tea in its whole-leaf form, when it is often fresher and of higher quality. A few ounces of a rare green tea is a relatively inexpensive luxury, and can make a tremendous difference in the teas you blend yourself.

——

To introduce guests to green tea, try this flavor-enhancer: To one teaspoon fresh lemon juice per cup of tea, add enough honey— about a half-teaspoon— to make it moderately sweet.

——

To Your Health Green Tea

Pat Dice

Before its health benefits were known, green tea had a hard time catching on in the West. Pat believes this is because the American palate deals poorly with bitter tastes. She formulated this tea to be a little bit sweet and spicy, a gentle introduction to green tea. Since its spices need to be simmered separately from the tea, however, it can't be blended in advance.

To brew 2 cups

1/2 teaspoon aniseed
2 cloves, coarsely crushed
1/4 teaspoon stevia
3 teaspoons green tea leaves
1 teaspoon chamomile flowers
2 cups water

Simmer the aniseed, clove and stevia for 3 to 5 minutes, or until the water is slightly greenish. Strain. Add green tea and chamomile to the strained, but still hot, liquid. Steep for 8 to 10 minutes. Strain again and drink warm.

Green Tea with Rosemary

Portia Meares

*p*ortia became acquainted with green tea a long time ago, while living in Japan. To this one, she added rosemary, whose tannin content contributes a flavor and color that recall black tea; the herb also contains antioxidants.

To brew 1 cup

1 heaping teaspoon green tea
1 6-inch sprig fresh or
   1/2 teaspoon dried rosemary
1 cup plus a few tablespoons water

To brew a 4-cup pot

4 heaping teaspoons green tea
2 6-inch sprigs fresh or 1 teaspoon
   dried rosemary
4 cups plus a few tablespoons water

Bring the water to a boil; add rosemary and simmer for 2 minutes. Remove from heat and allow to cool for 2 minutes. Strain into a mug or teapot (or simply remove the rosemary sprigs); add green tea, cover and steep for 5 minutes. Strain again, or serve complete with green tea leaves to be read later.

Long Day in the Texas Sun Tea

Susan Wittig Albert

Researchers are avidly investigating green tea's potential to lower the risks of skin cancer from sun exposure. Both Susan and her literary creation, China Bayles, live and garden in Texas, where the sun is hot and powerful. This green tea is packed with cooling lemon-flavored herbs, refreshing rosemary, and a little bit of ginger for spiciness.

To blend 50 servings

1/4 cup green tea
1/4 cup lemon balm leaves
1/2 cup lemon-scented geranium
  (pelargonium) leaves
1/4 cup lemon verbena leaves
2 tablespoons lemon grass
2 tablespoons rosemary
2 tablespoons dried, chopped ginger root

Combine herbs and tea in a glass jar. Store away from light for up to one year

To brew 4 cups

4 heaping teaspoons blend
4 cups water

Warm a 4-cup teapot. Heat water to a steady simmer; add water and blend to teapot. Allow to steep for 5 or more minutes. Serve warm, but not steaming hot.

Fire-Eaters Tea

Brigitte Mars

Brigitte designed this green tea to balance spicy foods, such as the pickled ginger and fiery green horseradish paste that accompany sushi. It could also complement a red-hot barbecue or curry dish. Peppermint and hibiscus are cooling; the marshmallow root protects and soothes the stomach. Jasmine adds an exotic scent and flavor.

To blend 48 servings

1/2 cup green tea
1/4 cup marshmallow root
1/4 cup jasmine flowers
1/4 cup peppermint leaves
1/4 cup hibiscus flowers

Combine tea and herbs in a glass jar. Store away from light for up to a year

To brew 4 cups

4 heaping teaspoons blend
4 cups water

Heat water to simmering; combine with blend in a warmed teapot. Steep for 5 minutes or longer. Strain if desired.

Stop and Smell the Flowers Green Tea

Susan Belsinger

Fresh lemon verbena leaves and rose petals make this tea smell like a luxurious garden. Susan recommends the apothecary rose (*Rosa gallica*) for aroma, flavor, and appearance, but any highly fragranced, unsprayed rose will do. In a pinch, you can use the flowers or leaves of a rose-scented geranium if there are no roses in bloom. Lemon verbena has a wonderful, sweetly lemony taste, but lemon balm or lemon grass also will do.

To brew a 4-cup pot

3 teaspoons green tea, or 3 tea bags
10 to 12 fresh lemon verbena leaves
Petals from 1 medium-sized, fragrant,
  unsprayed rose
4 cups water
Mild-flavored honey

Heat water to a simmer; combine with green tea, verbena, and rose petals in a warmed teapot. Steep for 5 minutes. Strain; add honey if desired (don't forget to close your eyes and inhale).

Chai

*I*f green tea evokes Zen simplicity, chai is a frenzied dervish's whirl. The word itself has multiple connections, meaning any kind of tea in Russian, and a very specific kind of tea in northern India and parts of Nepal and Tibet. Exotic spices, milk, sweeteners and strong black tea combine in traditional chai, making it strong, rich, heady and complex. But halfway around the world from its birthplace, in American and Canadian coffeehouses and homes, tea aficionados are creating new incarnations of chai.

Tea drinkers who first encounter chai in its native lands tell of visits to India, eating fried *pakoras* and drinking chai from newly-made clay cups. Some swear that the earthen cup imparts an inimitable flavor to the tea. The custom is to slurp the cup's contents, then smash it to bits on the ground—perhaps to signify enjoyment, akin to throwing wineglasses into the fireplace. Chai *wallahs,* or vendors, circulate through Indian trains, selling tea at every stop. Customers toss the earthen cups, called *kullarh,* out the trains' windows when finished.

Despite having traveled halfway across the planet, chai in the West remains as individual as those who make it. No two Indian restaurants serve the same kind of chai—and may it remain ever so! Even in commercially sold chai products, there is a huge amount of variation. You can buy chai in dry mixes or in bottles. Chai producers, often family business owners, sprinkle their packaging with puns, witticisms, or the lore and legends of the ingredients.

There are only three constants to chai: strong black tea, milk of some kind, and spices, usually including cardamom and ginger. Even the black tea is not a given—many formulators and manufacturers are developing decaf or medicinal versions. Some chais combine as many as a dozen different flavors, including cloves, cinnamon, anise or fennel seeds, black or white or pink peppercorns, allspice, nutmeg, star anise, and seasonings that have names only in one of India's many languages. Other chais are elegantly simple. The milk can be skim, two-percent, half-and-half, goat's milk, or, as one manufacturer suggests on the box, "soy stuff." In Nepal and Tibet, the drink may well be prepared with yak milk or butter. Debate joyfully rages about how sweet chai should be, whether honey or sugar should be used, and whether vanilla should be added to the milk. Should the tea itself be boiled, or is that a travesty? One aficionado asserts that the milk should be boiled—not once, but twice. The versions of chai gurgling forth from various coffeehouse chains are compared and critiqued, and chai connoisseurs can get downright steamed up over the propriety of using steamed milk.

Chai lovers do agree on one issue, however: the most splendid chai is the one you make at home. Producing chai can be a long labor of love, involving crushing spices individually and savoring their unique aromas. Or it can be as simple as adding ginger, cardamom, milk, and sugar to your customary cuppa. The contributors to this chapter recommend grinding whole spices in a mortar and pestle; doing so produces the strongest and freshest flavor. Powdered spices will tend to produce muddy, weak chai. Most recipes also warn against boiling the tea leaves, because this practice tends to make the brew too bitter. And we can't recommend trying to get a second batch of chai out of once-boiled spices; our results were unsatisfactory. A strong black tea tends to stand up to dilution with milk best, but if you are making chai with less milk or with none, you can probably get away with using a milder, subtler-tasting tea, such as Darjeeling or even oolong.

The recipes in this chapter only look complex. You can do a coarse grind of the spices, then combine them in a jar or resealable bag and store them in the freezer for several months. Or you can brew the spice/tea mixture and refrigerate it for up to three days; making chai then involves only reheating the mixture and adding milk. Once you've made chai a few times, the simmering and steeping and straining and warming become second nature, a set of hospitable rituals. And once the flavor of chai has etched its mark on your psyche, it becomes an indelible memory.

> **Producing chai can be a long labor of love, involving crushing spices individually and savoring their unique aromas. Or it can be as simple as adding ginger, cardamom, milk, and sugar to your customary cuppa.**

96

Quick Breakfast Chai

Yamuna Devi

This chai uses simple spices you may already have in the pantry. It also fills the home with satisfying scents.

To brew 1 large mug or commuter cup

1/2 tablespoon grated fresh ginger root
1/2 teaspoon cardamom seeds, outer pods removed
1 teaspoon crushed cinnamon stick
1 heaping teaspoon black tea or 1 tea bag
2 cups water or half water, half milk
Honey to taste

Coarsely crush the cinnamon and cardamom with a mortar and pestle. Bring the liquid to a boil. Add spices and tea bag; remove from the heat and steep for 3 to 4 minutes. Strain; serve hot.

Easy Masala Chai

Yamuna Devi

A *masala* is simply a particular blend of spices. There are many masalas; the spices involved in this chai are a classic blend, Yamuna says. The blending of masalas invites play; feel free to adjust the ingredients in this chai to make it your own.

To brew 2 cups

4 cloves
About 6 inches cinnamon stick
2 one-inch pieces fresh lemon or orange zest, or 1
*   teaspoon dried lemon or orange peel*
1 tablespoon loose tea or 2 tea bags of black,
*   peppermint, or chamomile tea*
2½ cups water
Milk, honey or sugar to taste

Coarsely crush the cloves and cinnamon in a mortar and pestle; add to boiling water. Cover, remove from heat, and steep for 10 minutes. Reheat again to boiling; add citrus zest or peel and tea. Cover, remove from heat, and steep for 3 minutes. Strain; add milk and honey if desired. Serve hot.

Dinner Party Chai

Robert R. Henderson

This chai goes well with long conversations after a dinner gathering. The ingredients, available in most supermarkets, are simmered, then strained; then black tea is steeped in the strained liquid.

To brew a large mug

1 slice fresh ginger root
2 whole cloves
8 whole coriander seeds
1 whole black peppercorn
1 1-inch piece of cinnamon stick
8 aniseeds
2 teaspoons strong black tea
1½ cups cold water
2-3 tablespoons milk
2 teaspoons honey

To brew 6 cups

3 slices fresh ginger root
6 whole cloves
1/2 teaspoon whole coriander seeds
1 whole cinnamon stick, crushed
3 whole black peppercorns
1/4 teaspoon aniseed
7 teaspoons black tea
6½ cups cold water
6-8 tablespoons milk
2 tablespoons honey

Coarsely crush the cinnamon, coriander, and cloves in a mortar and pestle. Place the water and spices in a saucepan; simmer gently for 10 to 15 minutes (do not boil.) Strain the mixture into a warmed teapot; add the tea leaves and steep for 3 to 5 minutes. Strain into cups; serve with milk and honey.

Never-Caffeinated Chai

Caroline MacDougall

*R*ooibos (pronounced ROY-bush) is a deep red herbal tea from South Africa that's available in some health food stores. Its body and flavor are similar to those of black tea, but rooibos is free of caffeine. This spiced rooibos tea comes close to the flavor of chai made with black tea.

To brew 6 cups

2 tablespoons rooibos
7 inches of cinnamon stick, shredded
A 1-inch piece of fresh ginger root, finely chopped
1 teaspoon chicory, roasted
1 teaspoon cardamom seeds
1/2 teaspoon black peppercorns
1 whole star anise
1/2 teaspoon cloves
6 cups water
Milk and honey to taste

Coarsely crush the spices in a mortar and pestle or coffee grinder; combine with rooibos in a 6-cup teapot. Add just-boiled water and steep for 10 minutes. Strain into cups. Add milk and honey to taste.

Refreshing Mint Chai

Yamuna Devi

In this blend, Yamuna combines some of the traditional chai spices with fresh or dried mint, and omits both the milk and the black tea. So is it still chai? Purists might sniff, but for those who must avoid both caffeine and dairy products, it offers chai flavors without potential stomach irritants. If fresh mint leaves aren't available, substitute three mint tea bags or two tablespoons dried mint.

To brew 4 cups

1 small cinnamon stick
1/8 teaspoon freshly ground nutmeg
1/2 tablespoon coriander seeds
1 teaspoon cumin seeds
4 whole cloves
1 teaspoon chopped fresh ginger root or
*   1/4 teaspoon dried chopped ginger*
1/2 cup fresh mint leaves, lightly packed
4 cups water
Honey to taste

Crush the cumin, cloves, and cinnamon in a mortar and pestle. Bring water to a boil; add the spices and simmer for 3 minutes. Remove from heat. Add the mint or mint tea bags and steep for 3 to 4 minutes. Strain into cups or a warmed teapot; sweeten with honey if desired.

Ginger-Orange Chai

Yamuna Devi

*F*or those who have a hard time with complex seasoning or who are allergic to some spices, Yamuna created a chai that's easy on the stomach. Fresh ginger is a sovereign remedy for mild digestive upsets. The only other spice is a small amount of cardamom.

To brew 4 cups

1/4 teaspoon crushed cardamom seeds
2 quarter-sized slices of fresh ginger root
3 one-inch wide strips of orange zest
2½ tablespoons (4 teabags) orange pekoe or
  decaffeinated tea
4 cups water or water mixed with milk
Honey to taste

Bring the liquid to a boil. Add the cardamom, ginger, and orange zest; remove from the heat and steep 4 minutes. Bring to a boil again, add the tea, cover and steep 3 to 4 minutes. Sweeten if desired and strain into individual cups or a teapot.

220-Volt Chai

Sheron Buchele

This is a "stayed up all night writing that presentation and need to be on fire to sell it today" chai. Or an "I've got three days of work to cram into the next five hours" chai. It packs a boot to the head and a bite to the tongue. If you're wondering why this and other chais are strained twice, it's simply to prevent the simmered spices from clogging the neck of your teapot.

To brew 4 to 5 cups

1/4 teaspoon whole cloves
1/2 teaspoon whole coriander
1/2 teaspoon dried ginger root (or 1/2 teaspoon
   chopped fresh, but do not use powdered)
1/2 teaspoon whole white peppercorns
1/2 teaspoon whole fennel seeds
1 teaspoon cardamom seeds
1 teaspoon whole allspice
1 teaspoon cut and sifted Siberian ginseng
1/2 teaspoon freshly grated whole nutmeg
1 whole star anise
3 sticks of cinnamon
3 cups cold water
1 heaping tablespoon of strong black tea leaves
2 cups milk
1/2 teaspoon vanilla extract
Sugar to taste

Coarsely crush the whole spices in a mortar and pestle in small batches; combine. Add spice mixture and water to a saucepan and bring to a simmer; cover and simmer for 10 minutes.

Add tea leaves to a warmed teapot. Pour the simmered spices-and-water mixture through a strainer into the teapot. Cover with a tea cozy or towel and allow to steep for 4 minutes.

Meanwhile, heat milk to just below simmer. Remove from heat and add vanilla.

Put 1½ teaspoons sugar, or more to taste, in the bottom of each cup. Fill halfway with tea, then top off with vanilla milk and stir.

Comforting Teas

Herbal teas are among the simplest medicines known, and sometimes the most effective for simple, minor complaints. They are also among the easiest to prepare. For mild stomachache, headache, congestion, oncoming colds, or sleeplessness, herb teas often work more gently than over-the-counter remedies, and get fluids into your system at the same time.

For this book, we asked herbalists to formulate teas that are not only healing, but taste good. Fortunately, many tea herbs have both these qualities. Licorice root, for example, is sweet enough to hide the taste of less palatable healing herbs. The root is also a powerful anti-inflammatory and stomach protectant that helps suppress coughs and even helps heal some ulcers. The same elderberries used to make wine are high in vitamin A and C; they're used here in a tea to strengthen the immune system and help stop a cold. The flowers of the same shrub have a lovely fragrance, and are used to ease coughs, colds and flu. Meanwhile, familiar peppermint and chamomile offer their flavors and benefits to many of the teas in this chapter.

Medicinal teas that contain no black or green tea sometimes call for slightly different brewing techniques. Some ingredients need to be simmered for a long time in order to release their healing components into water. Other herbs are more delicate and should not be steeped for longer than the instructions specify, or a bitter taste may result. If you are making only one cup of medicinal tea, try to cover your cup while the tea is steeping; doing so will keep the heat in, helping to make a stronger tea. The teas in this chapter can be brewed several cups at a time, stored in the refrigerator for up to three days and reheated as needed.

> The same elderberries used to make wine are high in vitamin A and C; they're used here to help strengthen the immune system and stop a cold. The flowers of the elder tree have a lovely fragrance, and are often employed in teas to ease coughs, colds and flu.

109

Upset Tummy Tea

Sheron Buehele

Both herbs in this simple, delicious tea are easy to grow, and both help soothe an upset stomach. Peppermint stimulates the digestive system; some herbalists consider it a balancing herb—one that fosters relaxation when you are tense, but boosts energy if you are tired.

To blend 40 servings

3/4 cup dried peppermint leaves
1/2 cup dried chamomile flowers

Mix thoroughly. Store away from light for no more than a year.

To brew 1 cup

1 heaping teaspoon blend
1½ cup water

Steep blend in just-boiled water for about 5 minutes. Serve hot or cold with honey to taste. It also makes a wonderful sun tea.

Headache-Easing Tea

Brigitte Mars

This tea combines soothing peppermint and chamomile with wood betony, skullcap, and white willow bark, three herbs traditionally used to relieve headache.

To blend 32 servings

1/4 cup peppermint leaves
1/4 cup skullcap herb
1/4 cup chamomile flowers
1/8 cup wood betony herb
1/8 cup white willow bark

Mix ingredients in a glass jar; store away from light for no more than a year.

To brew 1 cup

1 heaping teaspoon blend
1½ cup water

Steep blend in just-boiled water for 15 minutes in a teapot or French coffee press. Drink while warm.

Congestion-Clearing Tea

Maggie Oster

he only good thing about a cold is that it's a perfect excuse to stay home and drink tea. The menthol in peppermint and eucalyptus may help soothe sore throats and control coughing. Herbalists have long used elder flowers for coughs, colds and flu. Cinnamon and cloves give this tea a warming, spicy flavor. Maggie says breathing the steam of this tea is almost as soothing as drinking it.

To blend 28 servings

3/4 cup peppermint leaves
6 tablespoons elder flowers
6 tablespoons eucalyptus leaves, crumbled
2 tablespoons coarsely crushed cinnamon
2 tablespoons whole cloves

Mix thoroughly. Store away from light for up to a year.

To brew 1 cup

1 tablespoon blend
1 to 1½ cup water

Add just-boiled water and blend to a cup, teapot, or French coffee press. Allow to steep for 15 minutes. Strain if needed and drink warm.

Aching Heart Tea

Brigitte Mars

Who hasn't nursed a broken heart at least once? This tea combines hawthorn to improve blood supply to the heart; violet leaves, traditionally used as a cough expectorant; lemon balm, extolled by the British herbalist John Evelyn as "powerfully chasing away melancholy"; and other herbs to help ease depression, lift fatigue, and calm anxiety. Brigitte says it's perfect for sipping in the bathtub during a good, long cry.

To blend 36 servings

*1/4 cup hawthorn (mixed leaf, flower and
   berry)*
1/4 cup violet leaves
1/4 cup lemon balm leaves
1/4 cup oatstraw
1/8 cup motherwort

Combine herbs in a glass container. Store away from light up to a year.

To brew 1 cup

1½ teaspoons blend
1 cup water

Add blend to just-boiled water in a French coffee press, teapot, or covered mug. Steep for 15 minutes; strain if needed.

PMS Tea

Sheron Buehele

*T*his tea takes advantage of herbs you can grow or wildcraft if you don't want to purchase them. Dandelion leaf is a mild diuretic, but is also high in minerals, especially potassium. Cleavers (*Galium aparine*), also known as goose grass, was used to counter fatigue by a Greek herbalist of the first century A.D. Today it is used as a general detoxifying herb. If you wildcraft herbs, make sure that you are doing so from land that isn't sprayed with pesticides or other chemicals. Also be sure that you ask permission and know *exactly* what you are picking. If you do use fresh herbs, triple the quantity listed here.

To blend 36 servings

6 tablespoons lemon balm leaves
4 tablespoons chamomile flowers
2 tablespoons calendula flowers
2 tablespoons cleavers herb
2 tablespoons dandelion leaves
1 tablespoon mugwort herb
1 tablespoon sage leaves

Mix herbs thoroughly in a glass container. Store for up to a year.

To brew 1 large cup

2 teaspoons blend
1½ cups water
2 slices fresh ginger root
1 3-inch stick cinnamon

Put 2 teaspoons blend in a pre-warmed teapot or French coffee press. Pour in just-boiled water. Allow to steep for about 4 to 6 minutes. Put a stick of cinnamon and the ginger root slices into a mug and add steeped tea. Serve with honey to taste.

Post-Injury Tea

Brigitte Mars

F all off the mountain bike? Trip on some stairs? The body needs lots of TLC to repair bones, flesh, and cartilage after a sprain, strain, or other mishap. This tea is highly nutritious, helps to soothe inflammation, and gently relieves pain.

To blend 48 servings

1/4 cup nettle leaves
1/4 cup horsetail herb
1/4 cup oatstraw
1/4 cup alfalfa leaves
1/4 cup skullcap herb
1/8 cup licorice root

Combine ingredients in a glass container. Store away from light for up to a year.

To brew 1 cup

1½ teaspoons blend
1 cup water

Combine just-boiled water and blend in a French coffee press, teapot, or covered mug. Let steep for 15 minutes. Strain if needed.

Fight the Microbes Tea

Maggie Oster

Ever feel like microscopic invaders are using your body for a political convention? This tasty tea of immune-system strengtheners can help put a damper on the party.

To blend 9 servings

1/2 cup dried elderberries
1/2 cup dried honeysuckle flowers
1/4 cup chopped echinacea root
1/4 cup chopped astragalus root
1/4 cup chopped licorice root

Combine ingredients in a glass container. Store away from light for up to a year.

To brew 1 cup

2 tablespoons blend
1 cup water
1/2 teaspoon honey

Place the blend and water in a saucepan. Bring to a boil, then reduce heat and simmer for 20 minutes. Strain; sweeten with honey.

Healthy Dreams Tea
Pat Diee

Pat designed this tea to help those recovering from an illness. It includes linden flowers, an herb with a long tradition as a nerve tonic. Red clover is an expectorant; oatstraw is believed to help the body's efforts to repair itself, and licorice root soothes the stomach and helps the tea taste good. This is a good bedtime tea for children.

To blend 50 servings

1/2 cup linden flowers
1/2 cup red clover flowers
1/2 cup oatstraw
1/8 cup licorice root

Combine ingredients in a glass container. Store away from light for up to a year.

To brew 1 cup

1½ teaspoons blend
1 cup water
Honey to taste

Combine just-boiled water and tea blend in a teapot or covered mug. Steep for 5 to 10 minutes. Strain; add honey if desired.

The Contributors

Susan Wittig Albert, a medieval scholar with a doctorate in English literature, stepped down from the post of vice president of academic affairs at Southwest Texas State University to write and garden on land near Bertram, Texas. She is the author of the China Bayles mystery series and *China's Garden: Celebrating the Mysteries of Herbs.*

Susan Belsinger is a food writer and photographer whose work has appeared in *Gourmet, Food & Wine, The Herb Companion, The Herb Quarterly, Woman's Day,* and *The Washington Post.* She has written extensively on food and herbs with Carolyn Dille, including the books *Herbs in the Kitchen* and *Classic Southwestern Cooking.* Her most recent book, with Tom DeBaggio, is *Basil: An Herb Lover's Guide,* and her photographs appear in *Peppers 1998.* She lives in Maryland with her husband and two daughters.

Elizabeth Bergstrom owns Laurel Hill Farm, a family business in Haines Falls, New York, that includes an extensive garden of herbs and everlastings. Along with formulating herb teas, she handcrafts herbal giftware to sell wholesale to gift shops.

Sheron "Spike" Buchele has been a firefighter, international traveler, emergency medical technician and an environmental and safety coordinator for a national chemical company. But her first love has always been gardening and food. In 1994 she and her partner Curtis Rowland founded Fox Ryde Gardens, under which name they sell handcrafted herbal products. They also grow and wildcraft herbs on their land in the foothills of Colorado's Front Range.

Yamuna Devi is a food writer, teacher, gardener and lecturer on subjects including classic, contemporary and Ayurvedic Indian cuisines. She has taught culinary arts for the last 30 years, specializing in vegetarian food. She is the author of *Lord Krishna's Cuisine: The Art of Indian Vegetarian Cooking* and *Yamuna's Table.* She lives in Sedro-Woolley, Washington.

Pat Dice is a survivor of both cancer and systemic lupus who did her herbalism training with David Hoffman and a *curandero* elder. She is also trained in kinesiology and energy systems. She speaks, practices, writes and teaches in Northern Colorado.

Robert K. Henderson's articles have appeared in several national publications, including *The Herb Companion* and *Herbs for Health*. A wild herb specialist and rural historian, Robert has lived all over the world, usually in the middle of nowhere. His zeal for adversity springs from his Scottish and Western pioneer heritage. He and his wife live in British Columbia.

Sharon Lovejoy is the author and illustrator of *Sunflower Houses: Garden Discoveries for Children of All Ages* and *Hollyhock Days: Garden Adventures for the Young at Heart*. Her nature and gardening column, "Heart's Ease", is a regular feature in *Country Living GARDENER* magazine. Sharon is a dedicated organic gardener who tends plants in Cambria, California and South Bristol, Maine.

Caroline MacDougall began her career as an importer for Celestial Seasonings. She has since designed teas for The Republic of Tea, John Wagner's & Sons, and Yogi Tea. She now markets her own herbal coffee substitute, Teeccino. Caroline was inspired by a grandmother who owned a chain of New York coffee restaurants in the 1900s. She is a contributor to *Caffeine Blues,* by Stephen Cherniske M.S. She lives with her husband and two sons in Santa Barbara, California.

Brigitte Mars is an herbalist and nutritional consultant with more than 30 years in the natural medicine field. Her work has been published in such magazines as *Let's Live, Natural Health, The Herb Companion, Herbs for Health* and *Mothering*. Her first book, *Elder,* has just been released by Keats Publishing. She founded UniTea Herbs, an herbal tea company, and teaches and lives in Boulder, Colorado.

Portia Meares is an avid gardener who has written numerous articles on herbs for *The Herb Companion* and *Herbs for Health*. She founded an herbal business newsletter and was instrumental in starting the International Herb Growers and Marketers Association; she also served as its president for two years. She lives in Wolftown, Virginia.

Maggie Oster has written six books on herbs, including *Herbal Vinegar* and *The Herbal Palate,* in addition to books on garden design, perennials, Japanese gardens, and potatoes. She lives in Kentucky and gardens there and in Indiana.

Audrey Scano is assistant editor of *The Herb Companion* and production editor of *Herbs for Health* magazines, both published by Herb Companion Press. She lives with her husband, two dogs, cat, and rabbit in Loveland, Colorado. Concocting recipes with the herbs from her garden is one of her favorite pastimes.

Art Tucker, a well-known authority on essential oils and the taxonomy of herbs, is a research professor at Delaware State University in Dover, Delaware.

HERBS AND ACCESSORIES

Aphrodisia
62 Kent St.
Brooklyn, NY 11222
(800) 221-6898
Bulk herbs and spices. Free catalog.

Avena Botanicals
219 Mill St.
Rockport, Maine 04856
(207) 594-0694
Bulk herbs, organics.
Catalog $2.

Companion Plants
7247 N. Coolville Ridge Rd.
Athens, Ohio 45701
(614) 592-4643
Herb plants and seeds.
Catalog $3.

Elixir Farm Botanicals, LLC
Brixey, MO 65618
(417) 261-2393
Herb plants and seeds.
Catalog $2.

Frontier Herb Co-op
PO Box 299
Norway, IA 53218
(800) 669-3275
Bulk herbs, spices, teas and chai; tea accessories. Free catalog.

Horizon Herbs
PO Box 69
Williams, OR 97544
(800) 545-7392
Seeds for medicinal herbs. Free growing guide and catalog.

Jean's Greens
119 Sulfur Springs Rd.
Newport, NY 13416
888-845-8327
Herbs, containers, teas.

Mountain Rose Herbs
20818 High St.
North San Juan, CA 95960
(800) 879-3337
Herbs, including organics, herb seeds, and herbal teas.
Catalog $1.

Nature's Herbs
1010 46th St.
Emeryville, CA 94608
(510) 601-0700
Free catalog.

Pacific Botanicals
4350 Fish Hatchery Rd.
Grant's Pass, OR 97527
541-479-7777
Bulk herbs.

Rasland Farm
Rt. 1 Box 65 HC
Godwin, NC 28344
(910) 567-2705
www.alcasoft.com/rasland/
*Herb plants, scented
pelargoniums, and herb products.
Catalog $3.*

San Francisco Herb Co.
250 14th St.
San Francisco CA 94103
(800) 227-4530
www.sfherb.com
*Herbs, spices, tea and accessories.
Free catalog.*

TEA AND ACCESSORIES

**Barnes & Watson
Fine Teas**
1319 Dexter Ave. N,
Suite 30
Seattle, WA 98109
206-283-6948
*Blended fine teas, herbal and
scented teas.*

Camellia Tea Company
PO Box 8310
Metairie, LA 70011-8310
800-863-3531
*Their own blended and flavored
teas plus others; tea accessories.*

Celestial Seasonings
4600 Sleepytime Dr.
Boulder, CO 80301-3292
303-530-5300
*Herbal, green and black teas; tea
accessories; factory tours.*

**Chaiwalla Fine and
Rare Teas**
The Ashley Falls
Schoolhouse
PO Box 217
21 Clayton Rd.
Ashley Falls, MA 01222
*Green and black teas from India
and China.*

Choice Organic Teas
Granum, Inc.
2901 NE. Blakely Street
Seattle, WA 98105
(206) 525-0051
Fine and organic teas.

Dean & Deluca
560 Broadway
New York, NY 10012
212-431-1691
*Green, black, blended, and herbal
teas; gourmet foods.*

**Eastern Shore
Tea Company**
PO Box 84
Church Hill, MD 2163
800-542-6064
Fine fruited and scented teas.

**Equator Estate
Coffees and Teas**
5645 Paradise Drive
Corte Madera, CA 94925
800-809-POUR (7687)
Rare, blended, and packaged teas.

Freed, Teller & Freed
1236 Polk St.
San Francisco, CA 94109
415-673-0922
*Fine, blended, herbal, and flavored
teas; tea accessories and foods.*

Golden Moon Tea, Ltd.
PO Box 1646
Woodinville, WA 98072
206-869-5376
Fine and scented teas.

Grace Rare Teas
50 West 17th St.
New York, NY 10011
212-255-2935
Fine and blended teas.

Harney & Sons
Village Green, PO Box 638
Salisbury, CT 06068
1-800-TEA TIME
Fine and blended teas.

The House of Tea
720 S. Fourth St.
Philadelphia, PA 19125
215-923-8327
800-923-TEAS
Fine, blended, and flavored teas.

Imperial Tea Court
1411 Powell St.
San Francisco, CA 94133
415-788-6080
*Fine, scented, and organically
grown teas.*

Kado
The Way of Flowers
2319 N. 45th St., Suite 198
Seattle, WA 98103
206-409-0675
*Fine, blended, flower, and herbal
teas; tea accessories.*

Kinnells Scottish Tea
620 W. Seventh Ave.,
Suite 207
Spokane, WA 99204
509-747-9064
800-337-4832
*Fine and blended teas, tea
accessories.*

LiveChai
PO Box 7329
Boulder, CO 80306
(303) 442-6556
*Chai mix and ready-to-serve
aseptic boxes.*

MarketSpice
PO Box 2935
Redmond, WA 98073-2935
(206) 883-1220
*Fine, blended, flavored, and herbal
teas; tea accessories, spices.*

**Northwestern
Coffee Mills**
1025 Middle Road
Box 370
La Pointe, WI 54850
(800) 243-5283
Fine, blended, and flavored teas.

**O'Mona International
Tea Co., Ltd.**
9 Pine Ridge Rd.
Ryebrook, NY 10573
(914) 937-8858
Fine, blended and packaged teas.

Pannikin Coffee & Tea
1205 J St.
San Diego, CA 92101-
7082
(619) 239-1257
(800) 232-6482
*Fine, blended, flavored, and decaf-
feinated teas; tea accessories.*

Peets Coffee & Tea
PO Box 12509
Berkeley, CA 94712
(510) 704-8090
(800) 999-2132, ext. 220
Fine and blended teas.

**James Norwood
Pratt Luxuries**
1411 Powell St.
San Francisco, CA 94133
(800) JNP-LUXT
Fine teas and tea accessories.

Robert and Joseph, Ltd.
6281 Martin Lane
Redgranite, WI
54970-9533
(414) 566-2520
(414) 566-2275
*Fine teas, handmade tea bags,
do-it-yourself tea bags.*

**Royal Gardens
Tea Company**
PO Box 2390
Fort Bragg, CA 95437
(707) 961-0263
*Fine teas and tea bags, tea
accessories and gifts.*

Teahouse Kuan Yin
1707 N. 45th St.
Seattle, WA 98103
(206) 632-8689
Fine, blended, and flavored teas.

Mark T. Wendell Importer
PO Box 1312
West Concord, MA 01742
(508) 369-3709
Fine, blended, and packaged teas.

Additional Reading

About Herbs

Becker, Jim and Faye Brawner. *Scented Geraniums: Knowing, Growing and Enjoying Scented Pelargoniums.* Loveland, CO: Interweave Press, 1996.

DeBaggio, Thomas. *Growing Herbs From Seed, Cutting & Root.* Loveland, CO: Interweave Press, 1994.

Foster, Stephen. *101 Medicinal Herbs: An Illustrated Guide.* Loveland, CO: Interweave Press (in press).

Hawkey, Sue. *Herbalism: Using Herbs for Stress Relief and Common Ailments.* Lorenz Books, New York: 1997.

Kowalchik, Claire, and William H. Hylton, eds. *Rodale's Illustrated Encyclopedia of Herbs.* Emmaus, PA: Rodale Press, 1987.

Ody, Penelope. *Home Herbal.* New York: Dorling Kindersley, 1995.

Ody, Penelope. *The Complete Medicinal Herbal.* New York: Dorling Kindersley, 1993.

About Tea

Pratt, James Norwood, and Rosen, Diana. *The Tea Lover's Companion.* New York: Birch Lane Press, 1996.

Pettigrew, Jane. *The Tea Companion: A Connoisseur's Guide.* New York: Quintet Publishing Limited, 1997.

Rosen, Diana. *The Book of Green Tea.* Pownall, VT: Storey Communications, Inc. (in press.)

Index